COMPTOIR
LIBANAIS

A FEAST OF LEBANESE-STYLE
HOME COOKING

COMPTOIR
LIBANAIS

TONY KITOUS
& DAN LEPARD

THE OVERLOOK PRESS
NEW YORK, NY

CONTENTS

AN INTRODUCTION TO THE WORLD OF

COMPTOIR
LIBANAIS

AND LEBANESE-STYLE COOKING

Tony Kitous

Look, I am not a chef and I don't want to pretend that I am. I'm a self-taught, passionate home cook who adores Lebanese food. My love of Lebanese food is very simple. I enjoy sharing good food: food that's healthy, delicious, and, above all, simple and honest. And that's what this book is about. I wanted to share my passion, and I honestly believe that once you get close to Lebanese food, you'll want to share it with your family and friends, and you'll get hooked on it too.

YOU DON'T NEED TO BE A CHEF TO cook Comptoir Libanais dishes. This is food to enjoy: it's simple, it's fun, and it's easy to make yourself. It's a way of eating that I hope you'll want to embrace and make part of your lifestyle. It's friendly, it's often vegetarian, and above all it's affordable.

If I go back to when I was about 14 or 15, I didn't really have dreams for the future. I was a street boy. I was the type of boy who would go and hitch-hike, taking myself to the seaside, which was an hour away from where I grew up. I'd wake up and tell my dad I was going to visit my neighbor's family. My father naively believed me, so I'd hitch-hike to the seaside, then call him and say that my neighbors had asked me to stay for a week or two. Sometimes I'd stay a month and just call my dad and say, "They want me to stay longer," while I was really squatting in lots of different friends' houses at the seaside.

My holidays were my adventure time, and I had always been a boy who wanted to experience life. My father came from a

very humble family and I couldn't rely on him giving me pocket money, as that sort of money was almost non-existent when I was growing up. I grew up living next to one of the biggest football stadiums in Algeria and at that time my city had one of the best football teams in the country, and whenever they played it was a sell-out. So, when I woke up in the morning during match time, I'd buy 50 or 60 tickets, then I'd sell them back and make some money. I was brought up on the street and I wanted to survive. I used to make street food, like sandwiches with merguez and fries and a little harissa, and I would go and sell them at the football matches. My mother was my accomplice — she used to help me out making the sandwiches — and obviously my father didn't know that, as he didn't want people to think that his son sold things on the street. I was always independent and someone who had summer jobs. That has always been my life. I was never dependent on my father because it wasn't an option.

I arrived in London when I was 18 years old, and I came here on holiday. Yet 25 years later it still feels like I'm on holiday.

I just love what I do so for me it's been one long holiday and I've just been working from day one.

People ask me if I was shocked by British food when I first arrived. But right from the start I appreciated whatever home cooking I found in front of me. I was on holiday, enjoying myself, and like any student I was trying to find myself, eating different kinds of foods, travelling around London trying to explore it and find my place. At first I lived everywhere, staying in north then south London, until I eventually settled in the west.

I came to London with £70 in my pocket, and with that money I managed to find work and start my career. At no stage did I feel it was difficult. I came here with no expectations — it was simply a holiday. I remember the day I arrived, and my first night sleeping at Victoria Station. I remember it very well because there was a promotion for chocolate bars, which they were handing out for free in the station. That's something we definitely didn't have back home: we didn't give out free chocolates in the street. And I remember my friend and I getting two huge bags of the chocolates and we lived on them for a couple of weeks. And then for the following few weeks I was living on kebabs from the Turkish restaurants in north London. Looking back, it sounds crazy but that's where my fascination with food and restaurants began. Sometimes the food you try isn't all that good, but I ate everything, and a voice in my head said, "I can make this better." Perhaps it was my mother's influence, letting me think that with hard work and really good-tasting

With this book Tony Kitous brings his fast-paced and simple approach to the home cook, using evocative flavors and delicate textures inspired by the best food of the region.

food you can excite customers. That's what I've always strived for. And from those early days in London it has been work, work, work. But delicious work.

To my dearest Dad, Haj Chabane Kitous, *Allah Yarhamak*. Rest in peace. Just hoping you are next to me today . . . Missing you so much. This book is for you. Your son, **TK**

Introducing Comptoir Libanais

THERE ARE TWO THINGS ABOUT me that everyone knows: I love food and enjoy making food, and I love people too. I'm the type of guy who just loves meeting people, talking to people wherever I am. Looking back at my childhood, selling those sandwiches outside the stadium gates was a sort of "hospitality," and that interaction with people was just as important as the

"Keep your approach fresh and light, allow ingredients to retain their natural flavors"

product itself. You can't just say, "Here's a sandwich, give me your money." You have to challenge people with flavors and textures, open their minds to new tastes, and serve it with charm. Even if you're on the street you have to greet them as if you're in your own restaurant or your own home.

Why did I open Comptoir Libanais? I knew that if I was to stay in this country I'd better save up and open my first restaurant. And at 22, I did. It took four years of hard saving, some mistakes, and a mountain of support from friends, but I got a place off the ground and my approach to restaurant food started to evolve.

I've always had in the back of my mind the idea of doing a simple version of casual Lebanese dining, essentially a Lebanese canteen. It was just a matter of time before I was ready to do it, and when the time was right I opened Comptoir Libanais. I took the idea right back to basics and focused utterly on what I really wanted, what my friends wanted, and made that the goal. My vision of Lebanese food, which inspired Comptoir, is very much good food, good atmosphere, good design, and good value. So when we started Comptoir we made sure every single item, from the design to the lighting, the displays on the counter, the elements that made up our souk or retail bazaar, had relevance to Lebanese culture and to Comptoir. It was very important to me that we created something that wasn't pretentious, but was inviting, simple, and had something for everyone.

You can't do big ideas on your own, and it wasn't until I met Chaker Hanna, my partner in Comptoir, that we really began to create places to eat that were both friendly and relaxed, but with a huge

emphasis on bold flavors and freshness. Chaker brought a calm to my craziness, made me think about taking steps toward goals, and kept me sane and ordered when we had those days that seemed almost too difficult. And we share a passion for food. Chaker and I both eat at Comptoir daily, not just to ensure it's good but because — quite honestly — we love it. It just seems like the best place to meet and spend time with friends.

Living in London for the last 25 years has given me the opportunity to understand London culture, British culture, and European culture. But since I arrived here at such a young age I've wanted to stay in touch with my Arabic culture. I hope what we've done at Comptoir makes Lebanese

food and culture more accessible for the European customer, whether it's from our design, our service, or simply the attractiveness of the whole selection of food we present.

That's also what this book is about. Don't worry about where your inspiration comes from, or get distracted by having to search for the most authentic or most traditional Lebanese ingredients. Keep your approach fresh and light, allow ingredients to retain their natural flavors, and, most of all, enjoy the food you cook. I hope you will enjoy cooking these dishes as much as I've enjoyed eating them, but above all, I hope that they'll inspire you to play around with Lebanese flavors and techniques and have fun. **TK**

Lebanese food
by Kamal Mouzawak

Kamal Mouzawak is the founder of Souk el Tayeb, an extraordinary farmers' market in Beirut that brings together the produce grown by farmers and families from all over Lebanon. His world-renowned restaurants, Tawlet in Beirut and Tawlet Ammiq on the eastern slopes of Mount Lebanon, invite women from the villages to take charge of their kitchens with their home recipes, farm ingredients, and rare skills.

WHEN WE TALK ABOUT TONY'S COMPTOIR LIBANAIS AND ITS MIX OF Lebanese, Mediterranean, and North African cooking and influences, people often start to talk about food as being "Arabic" as an adjective. And I always wonder what that means. Is it being Muslim? I'm not Muslim myself and so much in Lebanon isn't Muslim. There are many Christian and Jewish people, so I don't think you can define Arabic food by religion. Is it the language? Well, I do speak Arabic but that doesn't mean I have lots in common with a North African or a person from the Arabic Gulf. Not all French or Spanish people have something in common as the same language doesn't necessarily mean they have the same background or traditions.

I think Arabic food is more defined by a region divided into three very distinct parts.

The whole of the Eastern Mediterranean is one part, so southern Turkey, the coasts of Syria, Lebanon, and Palestine, or what we call the Levant. Then there is the Arabic Gulf, which has a totally different climate. And third, there is North Africa.

When we talk about Lebanon we're talking about a very small country: 125 miles of coastline along the Eastern Mediterranean and 30 miles going inland, with Beirut in the center of that. And nearly all Beiruti come from villages outside the city in a similar way to that in which many New Yorkers or Londoners come from other places. But while many people in London or New York might have travelled a long distance from their first home to the city, in Lebanon you would only need to travel a maximum of 100 miles and you would be back in your village. And for many Lebanese their place of origin is the place they associate with the country's best food. The ingredients are the most flavorsome, and like Proust's madeleine, where food, nostalgia, and sentimentalism meld, their mother's cooking and their village's food and produce are always the best.

Is Lebanon a melting pot of different cultures? It's half Christian and half Muslim; half city people and half mountain people; half people looking to the east and half looking to the west. Geographically it's at a crossroads: if you look at it on a map it's like the belly of the Eastern Mediterranean. So many different civilizations and influences have left their mark on the tastes, traditions, and politics, and all of these things translate into a very diverse cuisine.

What has changed about Lebanese food over the last 30 years or so is the attitudes to food and cultural traditions. During the Lebanese civil war (1975–1991) the priorities were about surviving rather than safeguarding traditions or the environment. Following this, Lebanon looked to international trends and fast food, fast consumption, and fast agricultural methods began to proliferate. But in more recent times the Lebanese have rediscovered and repossessed their heritage, and we have seen the resurgence of traditional food production methods, cooking styles and dishes — as well as mouneh, the traditional method of food preservation. You now see more handcrafted food on sale, fruit conserves made with authentic home methods, tomato pastes cooked and bottled on small family farms, unusual varieties of olives cured in small batches rather than vast factory containers. This is what excites and inspires me today.

For me the dish that typifies the spirit of the Lebanese kitchen is tabbouleh. I have a journalist friend who compared tabbouleh to Lebanon. You can have a salad where you can see the tomato and the parsley and can separate them easily; or you can have them processed like you would a soup, totally mixed together, so you cannot separate them. With a tabbouleh you can very easily identify the ingredients but you cannot separate them. Lebanon is like that: a mix of so many different people, that together make up Lebanon but without one part would cease to be a whole community in many people's eyes. All of the ingredients make a tabbouleh, and if you take the prime ingredients out it ceases to be a tabbouleh. It's the definitive Lebanese dish par excellence.

Food for the Lebanese is a very important expression of affection, love, and emotion. Though I can't connect with our customers every day, every day I can share food with them, and that's a wonderful way of expressing similar feelings. Our pride is expressed through food. Look at our Sunday lunch mezze where the table is full of small plates of food. When you go to people's homes they always want to see your plate full. Food isn't a pill that you swallow in order to have your daily nutritional requirements; it's there to accompany the time you spend with family and friends. **KM**

ch 1. *Mezze* salads

Mezze salads

Sitting down for mezze—small plates of food—is as much about spending time with friends or family as it is about delicious food. It's about good conversation and cuisine melding into a feast at your table; dishes that excite and stimulate your senses.

The perfect mezze is essentially about generosity. Mezze fill the table, inspiring both your eyes and appetite. You're free from the formality of courses but can put different elements on a single table—there are no rules, no conventions, and you get to eat a bit of everything.

The next four chapters offer recipes for building your ideal mezze spread, but in your choice of dishes you should always find fresh, inviting salads and vegetable dishes. Insist on tabbouleh, the fresh green heart of every mezze, loaded with parsley, lemon, and tomato. Mix sweet with savory by combining fruits or pomegranate molasses with salad greens or dressings; and add color to your table with the vibrant fresh produce that is so abundant in Lebanese cuisine. ●

TABBOULEH

For me this salad is more about an abundance of hand-chopped fresh parsley and a scattering of tomatoes tossed with zingy lemon and olive oil dressing than it is about bulgur wheat. At Comptoir it's a dish I eat every day and I can't picture a good mezze without it. For the best results, get yourself some flat-leaf parsley that tastes crisp and peppery, and wait till you have tomatoes with flavor rather than making do with the bland, out-of-season offerings. Avoid using the food processor because it tends to pound the leaves too much. Honestly, take the time to make it, and the texture and flavor will be miles better.

SERVES 4 TO 6

2 very large bunches flat-leaf parsley

2 spring onions, finely chopped

3 to 4 firm but ripe medium tomatoes

1/3 cup (50g) dry bulgur wheat, soaked for 30 to 60 minutes in tepid water, then drained well

juice of 2 large lemons

1/4 cup (50ml) olive oil, plus extra to taste

salt, to taste

Pick all the leaves from the parsley but reserve the stalks: I add these to stock to give it a peppery bite. Then bunch the leaves up in handfuls on a cutting board and slice them evenly, trying not to crush the leaves. When they're evenly sliced, spread them in the middle of the cutting board and chop once more so you have an even "confetti" of parsley. Scrape this into a mixing bowl and add the onion, scattering it over the parsley. Chop the tomatoes into fine dice and add most to the bowl, reserving a handful to finish the dish. Add the bulgur wheat and stir: let stand for 30 minutes.

To finish, pour the lemon juice and olive oil over the salad. Sprinkle with a good pinch of salt, then toss everything together and carefully spoon into a serving bowl or serving board. Taste it to check that it's sharp and seasoned enough: it should be tart from the lemon but softened slightly by the oil. Top with the reserved chopped tomatoes before serving.

Other ingredients you can add are really up to you. Fresh mint chopped through with the parsley is good, and some people like it with cilantro, but that never tastes right to me. Do add more bulgur wheat if that's your preference, though I think it's best used sparingly in this dish.

COMPTOIR *tomato and halloumi salad*

This is my play on an Italian tricolore salad, using fried halloumi cheese stacked with fresh tomato then dotted with tender black olives and strewn with shredded mint. Rich, crisp, bright, and fresh. This is what I cook at home in the summer, and with a little olive oil poured over it becomes this extraordinary salad. High in calories? A little, but ever so good.

SERVES 4

10½ ounces (300g) halloumi cheese, cut into ½-inch (1cm) slices, marinated in fresh thyme, garlic and olive oil

1 to 2 large fresh tomatoes

⅓ cup (50g) pitted soft black olives, roughly chopped

small bunch fresh mint, shredded

olive oil

fresh lemon juice, to taste

Warm your serving dish.

Place the cheese slices on a plate and pat them dry with paper towels. Place a large, heavy-bottomed frying pan on the stovetop and get it moderately hot. Pour a little olive oil over the surface then place some of the cheese slices in the hot pan. Adjust the heat so the cheese turns golden and crisp on the base in about 1 minute, then flip the slices over, cook the other side, and scoop them out of the pan and onto the warmed serving dish. Do the same with the remaining slices.

Slice the tomatoes and layer them with the cooked cheese on the serving dish. Toss the olives over the surface and sprinkle with the mint. Then all you need to do is drizzle with olive oil, squeeze on a little lemon juice to taste — I like to be generous with the lemon — and serve. It's the sort of dish you need to eat immediately, so only make enough to just get your guests excited.

Other ways I like to serve it: sometimes I thinly slice 1 to 2 garlic cloves and place them in the base of a dish with the leaves from 3 to 4 sprigs of fresh thyme and a little oil. I put the slices of halloumi in the dish, flip them over a few times so the garlicky oil coats the cheese, then I leave them to marinate at room temperature for about 30 minutes, sometimes all day, before frying. This adds a subtle garlic-and-herb flavor that complements the tomatoes without tasting overly powerful. Delicacy is the key with this dish.

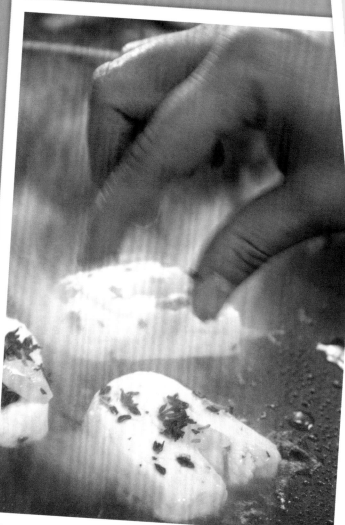

COMPTOIR TOMATO
and Halloumi Salad

BULGUR salad
with *fresh peas* AND MINT

There's one very simple healthy dish with bulgur that's evolved at Comptoir: a vividly green salad with mint and parsley, lightly cooked fresh peas, and pomegranate seeds for that bit of sweetness and crunch, mixed with a simple dressing of good olive oil and cider vinegar to bring out a much more interesting flavor. You can replace the bulgur with cooked quinoa if you want a gluten-free dish, and if I can't find really good pomegranates at the market I just use a combination of toasted sunflower seeds and chopped dried apricots or raisins. Not quite the same but it adds the crunch and sweetness I like.

SERVES 6

1 cup (150g) fresh or frozen peas

salt

2 cups (300g) dry bulgur wheat

freshly ground black pepper, to taste

small bunch fresh mint, leaves only, roughly chopped

small bunch flat-leaf parsley, leaves only, roughly chopped

1½ tbsp olive oil

2 tbsp (25ml) cider vinegar

seeds from 1 pomegranate

Simmer the peas for a few minutes in boiling water, adding ½ teaspoon of salt to bring out the flavor, then drain. Place the bulgur wheat in a bowl, cover with tepid water, and let stand for 30 to 60 minutes until soft, then drain well.

Chill the peas in a little iced water to hold their color. Fluff the bulgur with a fork and mix in salt and pepper to taste. At this stage the bulgur will keep in the fridge for at least a day, same for the peas, so you can make these in advance.

To serve, mix the herbs, drained peas, olive oil, and vinegar through the bulgur. Spoon the salad into a bowl, check the seasoning, then sprinkle with the pomegranate seeds.

Fattoush *with* POMEGRANATE MOLASSES dressing

Bread is a very special thing to me, a food I would never waste, and I'm sure this comes from my upbringing. So the fattoush salad, perhaps the most famous of all Arabic salads, brings together bread and green freshness in a way that is always a delight. The dressing I use mixes pomegranate molasses, a sharp, sweet syrup reminiscent of a sour treacle, with lemon juice and olive oil.

SERVES 4 TO 6

2 pita breads

olive oil, plus more to finish

2 tsp sumac

3 heads baby gem lettuce, chopped

small bunch mint, chopped

small bunch flat-leaf parsley, chopped

2 small cucumbers, diced

12 cherry tomatoes, halved

2 spring onions, chopped

4 to 5 radishes, thinly sliced

1 pomegranate (optional)

for the dressing:

¼ cup plus 1 tbsp (75ml) pomegranate molasses

scant ¼ cup (50ml) cider vinegar

1 tsp dried mint

2 tsp sumac

juice of 1 lemon

½ cup (125ml) olive oil

1 clove garlic, mashed

salt, to taste

Preheat the oven to 400°F (200°C/180°C fan/gas 6). Cut the pita bread into ½ to ¾-inch (1 to 2cm) squares and spread these out on a baking tray. Pour a little oil over them, then sprinkle with sumac and toss so they're lightly coated. Bake in the oven for 15 to 20 minutes, or until the pita squares have crisped and started to brown. Remove from the oven and set aside to cool.

Put the lettuce in a bowl with the herbs, cucumber, tomatoes, and spring onions. Scatter the radish slices over the top and sprinkle with the pomegranate seeds (if using).

Make the dressing by whisking the ingredients together in a bowl until smooth. Then add salt to taste. I like this dressing quite tart but play with the flavor to suit yourself.

To serve, simply pour about half the dressing on the salad, add the pita croutons, and toss everything together. Have the remainder of the dressing in a bowl on the table to serve alongside.

Stuffed GRAPE LEAVES

Warak Enab

This dish crops up in different guises from Greece to Iran, but this is the Lebanese interpretation. Delicious salty grape leaves are contrasted with pomegranate molasses, vibrant fresh herbs, and a hint of spice—everything you could possibly want in terms of flavor. Despite what you might think, stuffing and wrapping up the grape leaves is surprisingly easy, but the sense of achievement is immensely satisfying.

SERVES 6

about 16 ounces (500g) canned grape leaves in brine, or 20 to 25 fresh leaves

1 onion, finely chopped

2 large firm tomatoes, finely chopped

small bunch of flat-leaf parsley, roughly chopped

small bunch of mint, roughly chopped

½ cup (100g) risotto rice, such as arborio

scant ¼ cup (50ml) olive oil

juice of 1 lemon

3 tbsp pomegranate molasses

2 tsp dried mint

1 tsp freshly ground black pepper

½ tsp salt

2 medium potatoes, peeled and thickly sliced

extra chopped mint and tomato, optional

extra olive oil

Either wash the canned grape leaves in hot water then drain them and pat dry with paper towels, or cook the fresh leaves in salted boiling water for 1 to 2 minutes then set aside to cool.

Mix the onion, tomatoes, parsley, and mint in a bowl. Stir in the rice, olive oil, lemon juice, pomegranate molasses, mint, pepper, and salt. Toss everything together, then check for seasoning. If you like spices you could add some, but traditionally we keep the flavor natural and subtle.

Lay the grape leaves on your work surface one at a time. Squeeze 2 tablespoons of the filling with your hands (save any liquid that comes out) and place this in the center of the leaf. Fold the sides over and roll the leaf up tightly so the filling is trapped inside. Repeat with the remaining leaves.

Lay the potato slices over the bottom of a deep saucepan, top with extra chopped mint and tomato, if you like, then sit the stuffed grape leaves tightly together in layers over the potato.

Pour any remaining juices over and add enough water to the pan to keep the stuffed grape leaves moist but not swimming in liquid. Drizzle with a little oil, weight the stuffed grape leaves down with a plate, then bring to a boil on the stovetop. Reduce the heat to maintain the barest simmer (or use a heat-diffuser pad) and simmer very gently for about 2 hours until the rice inside the leaves is cooked. Set aside in the saucepan to cool completely, then drain off the juices from the pan and turn out onto a plate to serve.

GRILLED eggplant
with OLIVE OIL, **garlic,** *and mint*

This is one of those dishes at Comptoir that mixes my heritage with the sort of mezze I want to see on my table. You won't find this in Lebanon even though the cuisine is studded with extraordinary eggplant dishes. I eat far too much garlic, if that's possible, and the flavor of the eggplant and the pepperiness of garlic pair so well.

SERVES 4 TO 6

1 garlic clove

½ cup (100ml) olive oil, plus more to finish

2 large eggplants, sliced ½ inch (1cm) thick lengthwise

salt and freshly ground black pepper

fresh mint leaves and chopped fresh garlic, to finish

Crush the garlic clove roughly — not to a paste — and stir this into half the oil.

Heat a griddle or frying pan until hot. Brush the eggplant slices on both sides with the remaining oil, then place them on the hot griddle and cook until you start to see wisps of smoke from the edges. Check to see that they're starting to char without turning utterly black. Don't be afraid of them burning — you need to create the rich, smoky flavor. Once cooked, you can remove the eggplant slices to a plate, season with salt and pepper, then drizzle with more oil. When all the slices are cooked, sprinkle the top with chopped fresh garlic and a scattering of mint leaves.

This is a simple dish that you can get creative with. You can lightly spice the oil with ground cardamom, cumin, and cinnamon, or lightly sprinkle the grilled eggplant with spices while they're warm.

Other vegetables work well here, like zucchini, roasted peeled bell peppers, or peeled and boiled artichoke hearts.

FRIED ZUCCHINI WITH
YOGURT, tahini, and GARLIC

Really this dish is all about texture, so the crisp edges of the zucchini and the crunch from the fried garlic come through in the cool yogurt and tahini sauce. This is excellent served alongside simple grilled meats, or with grilled vegetables and soft bread. Though it's a simple dish it's best to eat it soon after it's made.

SERVES 6

vegetable oil, for frying

4 to 5 zucchini, cut into ¼-inch (½ cm) discs

½ cup (50g) all-purpose flour

4 garlic cloves, thinly sliced

¾ cup (175g) thick yogurt

scant ¼ cup (50g) tahini

2 tsp dried mint

salt and freshly ground black pepper, to taste

Fill a deep, heavy-bottomed saucepan with a 1½ to 2-inch (4 to 5cm) depth of oil, allowing enough space for this to triple in height during frying.

Dust the zucchini with the flour. Heat the oil then test the temperature by dropping in a slice of zucchini: it should cook until crisp and golden in about 30 seconds. Fry the remaining zucchini in small batches, allowing enough room so they can brown evenly.

Scoop the zucchini slices out of the oil with a slotted spoon, allow them to drain on paper towels and continue with the remaining slices. Next, drop the garlic into the oil, allow the slices to turn golden, then scoop out the garlic and drain it separately from the zucchini.

For the sauce, beat the yogurt and tahini together in a small bowl until smooth, then stir in the mint.

To serve, spoon the zucchini into a bowl and season with salt and pepper. Add the yogurt sauce and scatter the crispy garlic on top.

LAMB'S *tongue salad*

L'sanat

Tongue is a good thing, trust me. It seems strange to me that many people will only eat certain parts of the animal and discard the rest, even though, when you think about it, it's all the same beast. But for those of you who, like me, don't have those hang-ups, the delicate texture of lamb's tongue, once poached and sliced, is delicious. However, let me tell you that this warm salad tastes equally good with poached loin of lamb, kept a little pink and sliced while warm.

SERVES 4 TO 6

1 onion, sliced

2 garlic cloves, sliced

2 bay leaves

1 tbsp salt

4 cups (1 liter) water

5 or 6 lamb's tongues (they can usually be ordered from independent butchers) or 1 (½-pound/200g) boneless lamb loin, trimmed of fat

for the salad:

2 onions, thinly sliced

vegetable oil

large bunch arugula

2 ripe tomatoes, chopped

½ preserved lemon, finely sliced, or strips of lemon zest

Pita Croutons (see p. 32)

handful of walnuts

for the dressing:

juice of ½ lemon

scant ¼ cup (50ml) olive oil

1 tsp sumac

Place the onion, garlic, bay leaves, salt, and water in a large saucepan and bring to a boil. Reduce the heat to maintain a simmer and add the lamb's tongues or loin. Gently simmer the tongues for 1½ hours or the loin for 10 to 12 minutes for a medium-rare loin. Scoop the lamb loin out onto a plate when it's ready and then chill, covered, or leave the tongues to cool in the poaching liquid.

For the salad, place the onions in a small saucepan, cover with vegetable oil, and heat until the oil starts to bubble. Cook for 15 to 20 minutes over medium heat, stirring from time to time, until the onions are golden. Scoop them out of the oil and set aside to cool on paper towels.

Place the arugula in a large serving bowl or on a plate, mix with the tomatoes, then add the preserved lemon or lemon zest and scatter the croutons and walnuts over the top.

Carefully peel the skin off each lamb's tongue, slice the tongues, and poke the pieces into the salad. If using loin, slice the chilled cooked loin and add it to the salad. Sprinkle over the sautéed onions. Make the dressing by whisking the lemon juice and oil together, and spoon this over the salad to taste, then sprinkle with the sumac.

Fresh figs *or* PEARS WITH halloumi and arugula

Any time you see ripe figs, the sort that have a deep-red flesh and a fragrance, you absolutely must buy them. They're available for such a short time, but oddly you see them in the most unlikely places. In supermarkets you can sometimes find them perfectly ripe at very little cost; other times you pay a premium for them in the swankiest delis. You just have to keep an eye out. But otherwise, if I have some pears that have ripened in the fruit bowl at home they work rather brilliantly here. You can also use moist dried figs.

You can add more vegetables to this dish if you want to skip the halloumi. Roasted tomatoes glazed with a little pomegranate molasses and sprinkled with salt are excellent, as are green beans coated in tahini dressing and carefully spooned on top.

SERVES 3 TO 4

for the dressing:

scant ¼ cup (50ml) cider vinegar

1½ tbsp (25ml) olive oil

1 tbsp clear honey

2 tsp za'atar or sesame seeds

6 ripe fresh figs or ripe pears

9 oz. (250g) halloumi cheese, cut into ½-inch (1cm) slices

olive oil, for frying

large bunch arugula

salt and freshly ground black pepper, to taste

Make the dressing by whisking the ingredients together with a fork in a small bowl.

For the salad, cut the figs into quarters, or peel and cut the pears into good chunks, and toss with the dressing. Heat a large, heavy-bottomed frying pan, add a little oil, then fry the halloumi in batches until golden on each side. Keep warm on a plate while you cook the remaining cheese slices.

To serve, place the arugula in a wide, flattish bowl, strain the fruit, reserving the dressing, then scatter the fruit over the arugula and season with salt and pepper. Arrange the warm halloumi slices over the salad and spoon some of the reserved dressing over them.

Fried EGGPLANT
with POMEGRANATE MOLASSES

One of the great things about eggplants is the way they can give you different textures and flavors depending on how you cook them. Here we slice the eggplants thinly, salt and dry them to remove most of the moisture, then flash-fry them in olive oil to crisp them. The crispness offers a fantastic contrast when served alongside all the soft dips like hummus or muhammara, and tastes sharp and delicious with the sumac and molasses.

SERVES 4 TO 6

2 large eggplants
salt
olive oil, for frying
freshly ground black pepper, to taste
¼ tsp sumac
pomegranate molasses
fresh pomegranate seeds
small bunch of fresh mint, leaves only, finely chopped

Slice the eggplants as thinly as you can, aiming for about ¼ inch (½cm) thick, so use a sharp knife on a cutting board secured with a folded damp kitchen towel underneath, to stop it from slipping. Sprinkle salt over the slices so they release moisture, and let stand for 10 minutes. Take a clean kitchen towel or piece of paper towel and dry the surface of each slice on both sides.

Take a heavy-bottomed frying pan and pour in a ½-inch (1cm) depth of oil so you can shallow-fry the slices. Have a wire cooling rack set on a rimmed baking sheet ready on your work surface.

Next, heat the oil, then test an eggplant slice for temperature. You want it to fry to a rich golden brown on one side in about 30 seconds. When you're happy with the oil temperature, fry the slices 2 to 3 at a time, adding more oil and reheating the pan as you need to. Once the slices are golden on both sides, lift them out with a spatula onto the cooling rack and continue with the remaining slices.

When ready to serve, season the eggplant slices with salt, pepper, and the sumac, then stack the eggplant slices on a plate with a little pomegranate molasses between each slice. Sprinkle with pomegranate seeds and chopped mint to finish.

You could even add more spices to the eggplant, like ground cinnamon, cumin, or allspice with the sumac, if you like a more complex flavor.

LEEKS *with* TAHINI

Kurrat bil tahini

Baking the leeks in a dish in the oven helps to keep their shape, which is part of their beauty. I like to eat these at room temperature, together with simple lamb and pistachio kofta, grilled eggplant, and lots of warm, soft pita bread. They keep well in the fridge for a few days, if covered well, and any leftover cooking liquid is excellent added to soups or oven-baked dishes in place of water.

SERVES 4–6

8 leeks, ideally not too thick

3 or 4 bay leaves

2 garlic cloves, sliced

2 small sprigs thyme

½ tsp salt

freshly ground black pepper, to taste

olive oil

za'atar (or a mixture of dried thyme, finely grated lemon zest, and sesame seeds)

Yogurt and tahini sauce (see p. 38)

Preheat the oven to 350°F (170°C/150°C fan/gas 3½). Try to find leeks that are quite slender so you can serve them in chunks without having to halve them lengthwise. It's not a deal-breaker but to me it looks better that way.

Trim the ends of the leeks and cut them into 4-inch (10cm) lengths, rinsing them in cold water to remove any grit. Place them in an ovenproof dish, cover with water, then add the bay leaves, garlic, thyme, salt, and a little pepper. Cover the dish with foil and bake for about 45 minutes, or until the leeks are very tender when you stick the point of a knife into them. Set aside to cool in the dish, covered.

To serve, drain the leeks well and stack them in a serving dish. Pour a little olive oil over them, sprinkle with za'atar, spoon the yogurt and tahini sauce over the top, then sprinkle with more za'atar.

CURED *beef* with cheese

Basturma

This is one of those easy platters to put together. Much like the Italian bresaola, the cured beef we use here is called basturma. It's made by salting the meat, then squeezing out any liquid before rubbing a paste of spices into the surface. It has a deep rich flavor that suits soft cheeses and pickles. You can replace the basturma with bresaola or pastrami. They're not the same but they have a strong distinctive flavor. Or sprinkle slices of cooked beef with a mixture of ground cumin, fenugreek, chili powder, and paprika, and let sit for 1 hour in the fridge before serving.

A big part of the simplicity and ease of plates like this stems from the approach you can take to mezze. You want to present foods to your guests with pride, without the intimidation that exceptional or rare ingredients can often bring. Though I'll put time into thinking about what I want to serve at the table, I want that effort to be somewhat hidden when my friends and family eat together.

SERVES 4

pita breads

6 to 8 slices of basturma, bresaola, or pastrami

soft cheese, such as goat's cheese or salted ricotta

selection of pickles

fresh mint, to finish

za'atar, to finish

Preheat the oven to 400°F (200°C/180°C fan /gas 6).

Place the pita breads directly on the racks in the oven and toast for 5 to 8 minutes. When they're hot and just a tiny bit crisp around the edges, pull them out with tongs, place them in a basket, and cover them with a clean cloth.

Keep the meat in the fridge, covered, right up until the point you are ready to serve. Keep the cheese in the fridge until ready to serve as well.

Most pickles can be served in small bowls, covered, as they hold their moisture quite well like that, but if you want to present them on a big platter or wooden serving board, try to avoid plating them until just before serving. It might seem like a hassle at first, but, honestly, pickles start to dry out quickly and they're at their most delectable when there's a sense that they're in perfect condition and almost glistening with moisture.

To serve, arrange the pita, meat, cheese, and pickles on a platter or cutting board. Sprinkle with fresh mint and za'atar to finish.

OCTOPUS SALAD WITH chile

I know — there's a scariness when you first see octopus salad, but oh my word, it's so delicious and is one of my favorite mezze at Comptoir. Slow cooking octopus makes the texture very tender, and once it absorbs the lemon juice, olive oil, and chile flavors, it is simply magnificent. In my humble opinion, this is truly one of the world's great dishes. The other thing I love about it is that the dressed octopus keeps very well for a few days in the fridge. So when I get home late from the restaurant, having forgotten to eat as always, I can have it in the fridge, ready to tuck into with some hummus and pita.

SERVES 3 TO 4

1½ to 2 pounds (750g to 1kg) fresh or frozen octopus

¼ cup plus 1 tbsp (75ml) lemon juice or cider vinegar

2 large onions, roughly chopped

2 garlic cloves, chopped

2 tsp salt

for the marinade:

1 large lemon

1 to 2 tsp chile paste

salt and freshly ground black pepper, to taste

olive oil

to serve:

3 to 4 tomatoes, chopped

handful of flat-leaf parsley, roughly chopped

Get yourself a sharp knife and a cutting board secured with a folded damp kitchen towel underneath, to stop it from slipping. Cut off and discard the octopus head and beak, slicing it off just under the eyes, so that you're really only left with the legs held together by the skin at the top and a hole through the middle. Wash the tentacles well, stick them in a pot, cover with water, and bring to a boil. Simmer gently for just under 1 hour until the flesh is tender.

Stir the lemon juice or vinegar, onions, garlic, and salt into the hot liquid, simmer for 5 minutes more, then set aside to cool. Some cooks add everything at the start but I was taught that you'll get the octopus more tender if you add your flavoring at the end. Once the octopus is cool, discard the cooking liquid and chill the octopus, garlic, and onions until you need them.

The marinade is a cinch. Slice the cooked octopus tentacles into bite-size pieces and place them in a bowl. Cut a few strips of zest from the lemon and juice the lemon into the bowl. Add the zest and the chile paste to the bowl. Stir in the reserved onion and garlic. Season with salt and pepper, generously pour on some olive oil, then stir well and chill until ready to serve.

To serve, place the tomatoes in a bowl with the parsley. Add enough octopus to give you roughly a 50:50 mix, stir well, and serve. Keep any leftover dressed octopus in the fridge for 3 to 4 days.

ch 2. *Mezze* Dips

Mezze Dips

When thinking about Lebanese dips, I imagine many people will arrive at the most famous — hummus — but perhaps the fact that here is an entire chapter devoted to dips shows the range and versatility of this Lebanese mainstay.

Of course, I have included a recipe for the Comptoir's version of the creamy chickpea and tahini dip, but alongside it are dips to suit every palate and every occasion. Light and refreshing options, such as the Labneh (see p. 56), would make a perfect start to a meal where you've got heavier courses to come, while the Warm Lentil

Purée with Onions (see p. 66) is practically a meal in itself — the combination of rice and lentils making it substantial and filling. Served with bread and perhaps one or two of the mezze salads, you could leave the table feeling well fed.

Enjoy these dips as part of a mezze spread, as something to serve with drinks before a meal, or even as toppings for grilled meats or salad. I only ask that whichever route you choose to go down, you serve them with generous quantities of pita or flatbreads for maximum scooping potential. ●

LABNEH

Labneh is a staple you'll find throughout the Middle East. It looks very much like a soft cheese but is actually a creamy strained yogurt. Where on a British or American table you might find mayonnaise, in Lebanon you'll find labneh serving almost the same role. Now of course there are different opinions on how to make it, and the thing that always impresses me, when I eat it at friends' houses, is how small variations affect the flavor.

SERVES 4

2 cups (500ml) cow's-, goat's-, or sheep's-milk yogurt

salt, to taste, optional

a sieve, bowl, and cheesecloth, and somewhere cool to store it

Take a medium sieve or colander big enough to hold the yogurt but with a bit of depth to it. Set it over a bowl that will catch the whey that drains from the yogurt. Wet and then wring out a double layer of cheesecloth or a tea towel so that it's damp, and press it inside the mesh of the sieve.

Some cooks like to salt the labneh at this point — I don't — but if you like, just stir a little salt in with the yogurt to taste, remembering that it will intensify in flavor as it drains. Pour the yogurt into the lined sieve and leave it undisturbed in the fridge overnight. At first you might think that it's draining so slowly that nothing is happening, but have faith. Overnight the liquid will drip away and leave a condensed yogurt that's much thicker, smoother, and cheese-like. Serve the labneh right away or store it in the fridge, covered, for up to a week.

Labneh with black olives & MINT

SERVES 4

handful of black olives, pitted and chopped

1 recipe labneh (see above)

chopped fresh mint

olive oil

Simply stir chopped pitted olives into the labneh, spoon it into a bowl, and top with more olives, a sprinkling of chopped fresh mint, and a drizzle of olive oil. Really the proportions are up to you but I like it so that there are a few pieces of olive in every spoonful without it overpowering the creaminess of the labneh.

LABNEH with VEGETABLES

SERVES 4

1 cucumber, chopped into fingers
1 recipe labneh (see p. 56)
chopped fresh mint
za'atar

On its own, labneh makes a great simple dressing for raw or cooked vegetables. Mix the cucumber with enough labneh so it's just coated, then served with a little fresh mint and za'atar sprinkled over it. This dish is delicious alongside grilled chicken. Sliced radishes, turnips, or kohlrabi are equally good this way.

LABNEH *balls preserved* **in olive oil**

SERVES 4

1 recipe labneh (see p. 56), drained for 2 to 3 days, until firm enough to roll into balls

olive oil

Sterilize a 1-quart (1-liter) jar and its lid by washing, rinsing, and drying them, then heating them in the oven to 300°F (140°C) for 10 minutes. Let cool in the oven before filling and sealing as directed below.

Take small pieces of the drained labneh and roll them into balls about the size of an unshelled walnut, and then leave these to dry slightly in the fridge overnight on a tray lined with paper towels.

The next day, stack the labneh balls in the sterilized jar, cover completely with olive oil, and close with a very clean lid. Leave at room temperature for 2 weeks before using. The labneh balls will sour and become firmer, and will take on some of the olive flavor. You can also roll the labneh balls in sumac, black sesame seeds, or za'atar before preserving them in oil.

LABNEH *with* za'atar (OR HERBS)

Labneh bil za'atar

SERVES 4

1 recipe labneh (see p. 56)
olive oil
za'atar or herbs

This is the most basic variation, and really just involves spooning labneh into a bowl, swirling the top with a spoon, then pouring olive oil over the top and sprinkling with za'atar before serving.

If you don't have za'atar, you can sprinkle chopped herbs, such as dried thyme, on the labneh instead, together with some grated lemon zest and toasted sesame seeds. In addition, I like to add some sliced mint and serve it with sticks of fresh unpeeled cucumber on the side as an alternative to bread.

Labneh *with* BEETS

Labneh bil shoumandar

SERVES 4

1 recipe labneh (see p. 56)
1 bunch fresh beets, trimmed
2 to 3 tbsp tahini

This is probably one of the most psychedelic ways to serve labneh as the bright pink color looks almost artificial. But wow, the flavor has a complexity that almost hides its simplicity. I like to roast the beets in their skins, let them cool, then peel, chop, and purée the beets until almost smooth. Then I blend the mixture — about 1 part beet purée to 2 parts labneh — in the bowl of a food processor until smooth, with a few tablespoons of tahini to thicken it. It's excellent served with roast or grilled lamb.

Warm LENTIL
purée with onions

Moujadara

In the Lebanon this simple dish is traditionally made with slow-cooked rice and lentils, to give it a creamy texture. Often served with fried onions, probably a later addition to this ancient dish, it's a delicious warm mezze that adds a rich savory character to even the simplest vegetarian menus. You could stir pieces of chopped grilled lamb through it, or just serve some alongside it. A beautiful and warming dish which will soothe and reassure you after a long day.

MAKES 4 TO 6 LARGE SERVINGS

4 large onions

3 tbsp olive oil, plus extra for frying

salt

²/₃ cup (125g) brown lentils

¹/₃ cup (75g) risotto rice, such as arborio, or brown rice

freshly ground black pepper, to taste

Peel and slice 3 of the onions and place them in a saucepan with the olive oil, a good pinch of salt, and a splash of water. Cook over medium heat until the onions are translucent and the moisture has evaporated. Then increase the heat and cook, stirring often, until the onions caramelize, turn a rich golden brown, and are almost burning.

Stir in the lentils, add about 1 cup (250ml) water, then bring to a boil and simmer until the lentils start to break down, adding more water as needed. This helps to give a creamy texture. Purée the lentils in a food processor with enough cooking liquid (reserve any extra) to create a smooth creamy consistency then return this to the pot and add the rice. Cook until the rice is just on the edge of breaking up, stirring often as you would a risotto. At this point you can store the lentil mixture in the fridge, covered, for 3 to 4 days.

To serve, heat about ¼ cup (75ml) of olive oil in a small, heavy-bottomed saucepan. Slice the remaining onion and cook until browned and beginning to crisp. Scoop them out with a slotted spoon, discard the oil (though you can use it again for frying other dishes), and set aside to cool. Reheat the lentil purée, season with salt and pepper to taste, then serve in a bowl with the onions sprinkled over the top.

If you like, you can add spices with the rice, like a little cumin and cinnamon or even a little chile, but there is a beauty in the simple flavor of the lentils and onions that I prefer.

Comptoir **hummus**

Our hummus is strongly flavored with lemon, garlic, and tahini so it's much more intense than the sort you get from the supermarket. If you want, you can remove the skin from the chickpeas first. If someone does it for me, then I love it as the flavor is better, but if it's just me, I'm lazy and leave them on. If you purée the chickpeas first, it's easier to get that authentic smooth texture, which I prefer.

SERVES 4 TO 6

1 ¹/₃ cup (225g) drained cooked chickpeas, cooking liquid reserved

¼ cup plus 1 tbsp (75ml) fresh lemon juice

1 to 2 garlic cloves, crushed

²/₃ cup (150g) tahini (store-bought, or homemade, see p. 230), stirred until creamy before measuring

¾ tsp salt, or to taste

pinch of ground cumin (optional)

Purée the warm chickpeas with the lemon juice, garlic, and about ¼ cup (50ml) of the chickpea cooking liquid or water in a blender until it's as smooth as you can get it, using extra cooking liquid or water if needed.

Put the tahini in a mixing bowl, add a third of the chickpea purée, and whisk it in. At first the tahini will seize, but gradually whisk in more and more of the chickpea purée until the hummus is the consistency you like. If the mixture is slightly thick, beat in a little water or lemon juice to soften it. Finally, beat in the salt and, if you like, a pinch of cumin.

An even simpler way to make hummus is to place cold drained chickpeas in a food processor with half the lemon juice and a mashed clove of garlic then process until smooth. Next, add half the tahini, then process again until very smooth. You can add 1 or 2 small ice cubes to the mixture with the tahini to create a very pale color. Then add more garlic, tahini, or lemon juice and salt to taste.

COMPTOIR *Hummus*

Smoked EGGPLANT purée
with garlic, tahini, AND MINT

Baba ghanoush

The secret to achieving great flavor and texture in this simple mixture of cooked puréed eggplant, sesame paste, and strained yogurt is allowing moisture to evaporate and concentrate the eggplant. When you get it right, you end up with an outrageously complex dish that defies easy explanation. To be honest, the tweaks you can make to this dish while still keeping it pure are many. The way you add the garlic, the type of yogurt used, the way you spice it or not — all contribute to the unique signature each cook brings to their baba ghanoush.

To get the best flavor, you want to grill the eggplant over an open flame until the flesh is soft. So I char the skins over the flame of a gas stovetop, then bake them in the oven with the garlic until tender. A friend of mine likes to char and bake an onion at the same time, and chops the soft onion through the mixture.

SERVES 4 TO 6

2 eggplants, about 1 pound (500g)

2 to 3 garlic cloves, unpeeled

1 tsp salt

¼ cup plus 1 tbsp (75g) tahini (store-bought, or homemade, see p. 230), stirred until creamy before measuring

1½ tbsp (25ml) olive oil

scant ¼ cup (50g) labneh (see p. 56) or thick yogurt

chopped mint, pomegranate seeds, and sumac, to finish

Preheat the oven to 400°F (200°C/180°C fan/gas 6).

Prick the eggplants with a fork and sit them over the flame of a gas stovetop to char the skin, rotating them so all sides get charred, then place them on a baking sheet with the garlic and bake for about 40 minutes, until collapsed and very soft. Alternatively, place under a broiler or on a grill with the garlic and cook until both are soft inside and the skin of the eggplants is charred.

Split the eggplants open on a cutting board, scoop out the soft flesh, and discard the skin, then place the flesh in a colander set over a bowl. Peel the garlic. Add half the salt to the eggplant, stir well, and let stand for 15 minutes to let any excess liquid drain away. Then return the flesh to the cutting board along with the soft garlic and finely chop. Discard any liquid from the bowl, place the chopped eggplant and garlic in it, and stir in the remaining salt, along with the tahini and oil, until thick. Add the labneh, then spread the baba ghanoush around the bowl with a spoon and sprinkle with mint, pomegranate seeds, and sumac to finish.

ROASTED peppers, nuts, chile, AND CUMIN

Muhammara

The version of this classic Arabic mezze I prefer at Comptoir is more heavily spiced and coarser than those you might traditionally find in Lebanese restaurants, but it's the one I like best. Having said that, I've eaten it so many different ways in Beirut, prepared both by home cooks and in restaurants, that it's almost an excitement just to see what spin each cook puts on it. Essentially this dish is a purée of roasted red peppers, oil, spices, and nuts, sharpened with a syrup made from pomegranates that adds a tart flavor reminiscent of lemons. To be honest, I like it made with a mixture of nuts, something that might shock purists, but combining roasted walnuts, cashews, pine nuts, and pistachios suits my taste. It keeps very well in an airtight container in the fridge, and once you get a taste for it, it becomes utterly addictive.

SERVES 4 TO 6

2-3 large red bell peppers

olive oil

8 ounces (250g) mixed shelled unsalted nuts, like walnuts, almonds, cashews, etc., plus extra to finish

½ tsp ground cumin

For the peppers:

2 garlic cloves, mashed

1 tbsp chile paste

1 tsp ground cumin

1 tbsp ground paprika

2 tbsp pomegranate molasses

tomato paste, optional

salt, to taste

Preheat the oven to 425°F (220°C/200°C fan/gas 7). Start by roasting the peppers. Place them on a baking sheet, drizzle with a little olive oil, and roast in the oven for about 15 minutes, until the skins are blackened and charred. Meanwhile, place the nuts on a separate baking sheet, drizzle them with oil and sprinkle with the cumin, then roast for 15 minutes, until gently toasted.

Peel and deseed the peppers, then place them in the bowl of a food processor with a scant ¼ cup (50ml) olive oil and the garlic, chile paste, cumin, paprika, and pomegranate molasses and blend until almost smooth. If you prefer the color to be the deepest red, you can add a little tomato paste. Season with salt to taste, thin the consistency with a little water, if needed, and spoon into a bowl to serve with extra nuts sprinkled over the top, if you like.

ch 3. *Mezze* Baked & Fried

Mezze Baked & Fried

This chapter is all about the "wow" factor of pastries and the pleasure we all derive from biting into an irresistibly crisp shell to discover the inviting, undoubtedly rich and luxurious filling that lies inside.

The dough used to make the traditional triangular-shaped fatayer and sambusak pastries is light, crisp, and thin. But let's face it — the star of a pastry really isn't the pastry itself, it's the contents. Many savory pastries in Lebanon are based around cheese, but you'll also find meat, chicken, or vegetable fillings, all topped with herbs and spices for an intense hit of flavor. This chapter also introduces you to what could almost be described as Lebanon's national dish — kibbeh. Kibbeh are small, round or torpedo-shaped balls made from a crust of ground meat and bulgur wheat ground up with spices, which contain a filling of more meat, nuts, and spices.

It may sound strange, but the countless interpretations you'll find across the whole of the Arab world speak for themselves — to me, kibbeh is comfort food at its best.

Sambusak *or* FATAYER *pastry*

Little pastries filled with a variety of ingredients, from chopped herbs and soft cheese to meat, walnuts, or chicken, can be found throughout the Arab world, under different names. These cheeky little savory parcels have a delicious filling tucked inside and can be served either hot or cold. They freeze well, and because they're so small they can be reheated easily.

You want a flour that produces a dough that stretches easily, and bread flour will do that. However, this can make the pastries a little tough and not as tender as the ones we have at Comptoir. If you want to experiment, use half bread flour and half all-purpose flour or half Italian pasta flour, as this will give a more tender result.

MAKES 12 OUNCES (350G) DOUGH

½ cup (125ml) warm water

1 ½ cups (200g) bread flour, plus extra for kneading

1½ tbsp (25ml) olive oil

1 tbsp superfine sugar or clear honey

1 tsp salt

Pour the water into a bowl, then add the flour, olive oil, sugar or honey, and salt and mix everything together well. Aim for a firm-ish dough, adding more water or flour to get the texture you want. Cover the bowl with plastic wrap, set aside for 10 minutes, and then lightly knead the dough. Return it to the bowl, cover again, then set aside for about 1 hour at room temperature and it's ready to use. If you want to make the dough ahead of time, you chill it at this point, then leave it at room temperature for 1 hour before shaping.

Some basic tips for making the best pastries: roll the dough very thin, otherwise you end up with too much pastry surrounding the filling. I use a little flour, as oil sometimes stops the edges from sealing firmly, but figure out what works best for you. The dough will keep well in the fridge for a few days, and gets easier to roll, but it will change color and go slightly gray. This is just the flour oxidizing and it won't affect the flavor. You can also freeze the dough. Simply thaw it and return it to room temperature before using.

SAMBUSAK *filled* with cheese and MINT

Sambusak bil jabneh

These small turnovers are excellent served with a glass of arak or lemonade in the afternoon. At Comptoir we use a cheese called akkawi; its flavor and melting character are a little like halloumi. If you can't get akkawi or halloumi, you could use firm, drained mozzarella, but try for halloumi. I know that we're often told that fresh herbs beat dried every time, but in countries where the summers are extremely hot, dried herbs will usually have a place in the kitchen. And though it might sound strange at first, the flavor of dried mint is perfect in these cheese pastries.

MAKES ABOUT 20 SMALL SAMBUSAK

1 recipe Sambusak Pastry (see p. 82)

flour or oil, for rolling the dough, plus extra oil for frying

for the cheese and mint filling:

5 ounces (150g) halloumi, sliced

5 ounces (150g) feta cheese, crumbled

1 egg, beaten

small bunch of fresh mint, or 2 tsp dried

for the olive and thyme filling:

5 ounces (150g) halloumi, grated

5 ounces (150g) feta cheese, crumbled

1 tsp chile paste

1 tsp dried thyme

¾ cup (100g) pitted black olives, roughly chopped

Start by preparing and resting your pastry dough (see p. 82). There are two ways to cook these sambusak: frying or baking. If you'd like to bake them, preheat the oven to 400°F (200°C/180°C fan/gas 6).

If you're making the cheese and mint filling, soak the halloumi in cold water for a few hours. Pat the cheese dry and grate it into a bowl. Add the crumbled feta, mint, and beaten egg, and mix until well combined. If you're making the olive and thyme filling, just stir the chile paste and thyme into the cheeses, then stir in the olives.

Divide the dough into ½-ounce (15 to 20g) pieces and form them into balls. Place them on an oiled baking sheet, cover, and let rest for 15 minutes. Roll one ball out on a lightly floured or oiled surface to about ⅛ inch (3mm) thick, then place 1 to 2 teaspoons of the filling in the middle and brush a little water around the edges. Fold the dough over, then seal the edges firmly by crimping them with a fork. Repeat with the remaining dough and filling.

Either brush the sambusak with olive oil and bake on a baking sheet lined with parchment paper for 20 to 25 minutes until puffed and golden, or to fry, pour a 1-inch (3cm) depth of oil into a deep, heavy saucepan and heat until a scrap of dough puffs and turns golden in about 1 minute. Fry the sambusak in batches, turning them once, until golden and puffed, then set aside to cool on a baking sheet lined with paper towels while you fry the remainder.

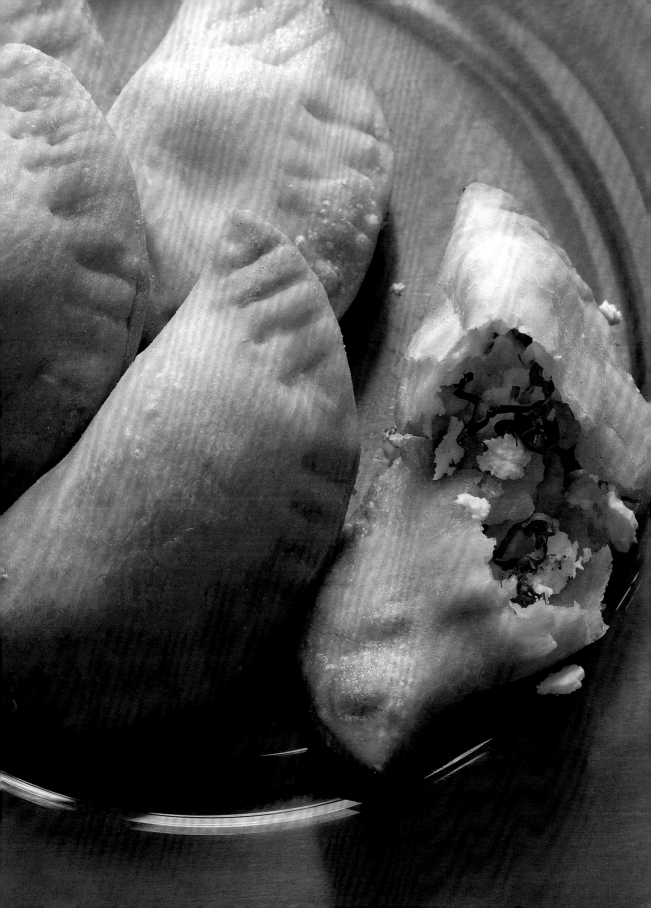

RAKAKAT *with chicken* and SUMAC

Rakakat lahma

Traditionally these are made with cheese or lamb, but chicken pastries are becoming more common. I like to use thin sheets of pastry, in reality a kind of crêpe, called feuilles de brick, which resemble a very white, slightly firm pancake. Although they are becoming more widely available in supermarkets, they can be quite hard to find, so when I do find them, I keep a batch in the freezer. If you can't get ahold of them, you could use phyllo pastry. Once fried, they keep well in the fridge but if you try to make them ahead without cooking them, the pastry can look a little rough.

MAKES ABOUT 24 RAKAKAT

olive oil, for frying

2 large onions, sliced

1 lb. (500g) chicken meat (thigh or breast), skinned, boned, and finely chopped

1 tsp ground cinnamon

1 tsp sumac

¾ cup all-purpose flour, to seal

12 sheets of feuilles de brick or phyllo pastry

salt and freshly ground black pepper, to taste

Heat about ¾ inch (2cm) of oil in a medium, deep saucepan, add the onions, and cook until they are a rich golden brown. Use a slotted spoon to scoop the onions out into a colander set over a bowl, and set aside. Let the oil cool, then pour most of it into a jug to use when deep-frying later, leaving 2 to 3 tablespoons in the pan.

Heat the pan again, add the chicken, and cook until it begins to color. Season well with salt and pepper, then stir in the spices. Remove from the heat, mix in the sautéed onions, and set aside to cool.

Mix the flour with enough water to make a thin paste. This will be used to seal the rolls. Take a sheet of pastry, slice it in half, and at one end spoon a line of 1 to 2 tablespoons of the filling. Fold in the edges over the filling, then roll up tightly, leaving about ½ inch (1cm) at the end. Rub this exposed end with the flour paste, then press it down to seal. Place the sealed rakakat on a plate or tray while you roll the remainder.

Place the reserved oil in a heavy-bottomed saucepan, adding more as needed to make sure you have 1 to 1½ inches (3 to 4cm) of oil in which to fry the rakakat. Heat the oil over medium heat, and once you think the oil is hot, add one of the rakakat to test the temperature: it should turn a light golden brown in 1½ to 2 minutes. Once you've gotten the temperature right, fry the rakakat in batches, turning them, until golden all over, then drain on paper towels briefly before serving while still warm.

FATAYER *with cheese* and spinach

Fatayer are usually triangular-shaped pastries, either sealed at the top or left open. Sealing the edges of the pastry at the top protects the filling so it's perfect or you can leave the top open the way we do at Comptoir and pinch the edges of the filled fatayer to form a triangular shape as in the photo here. If you sprinkle a deep layer of cheese on top before baking, any filling underneath is protected from the heat of the oven, allowing the pastry to be crisp but the filling soft.

MAKES ABOUT 20 SMALL FATAYER

1 recipe Sambusak Pastry (see p. 82)

flour or oil, for rolling the dough

for the filling:

2 tbsp olive oil

1 pound (500g) baby spinach

½ cup (50g) walnuts, chopped

2 tbsp pomegranate molasses

5 ounces (150g) halloumi or mozzarella, drained and grated or finely chopped

5 ounces (150g) feta cheese, crumbled

small bunch fresh mint, leaves only, chopped

black onion (nigella) seeds or za'atar, to finish

Start by preparing and resting your dough (see p. 82). Preheat the oven to 350°F (180°C/160°C fan/gas 4). Line a few baking sheets with parchment paper.

Make the filling by heating the olive oil in a large frying pan until smoking hot, then add the spinach and fry quickly until it just begins to wilt. Tip the spinach into a colander and set aside to cool, then squeeze the cooked spinach as hard as you can to remove the liquid. Chop the spinach, then place it in a bowl with the walnuts and pomegranate molasses, and mix well.

Chop the dough into small pieces, about the size of an unshelled walnut, then shape these into balls and set aside to rest on an oiled plate, covered, for 15 minutes (this makes rolling easier).

Roll out each dough ball on a lightly floured or oiled surface to about 3 inches (8cm) wide. Place a heaping teaspoon of the spinach filling in the center of one, then with the tips of your fingers rub a little water around the bare edges of the dough. At 3 equal points, pull the dough up ½ to ¾ inch (1 to 2cm) and pinch the dough together to seal — you should have created a protruding edge around the filling.

Spread the cheese over the filling, then top with a pinch of mint, sprinkle with the black onion seeds or za'atar, and place on the lined baking sheets. Repeat with the remaining dough and filling, then bake for about 30 minutes, until crisp and golden, rotating the baking sheets if one batch looks like it is browning more quickly.

BAKED sambusak *with* potato AND CHEESE

Baking these turnovers gives quite a different flavor than frying, especially with the seeds on top, which toast in the heat of the oven. The filling is simple to make but the resulting sambusak have a deep, complex flavor. You can use cooked, drained chickpeas instead of the potatoes: just mash them a little before mixing them into the filling. When we make these at Comptoir, we get a few of the chefs working together and suddenly the task of making lots of sambusak doesn't seem as daunting. You can talk, help each other, and it becomes something that's a little fun to do.

MAKES ABOUT 20 SAMBUSAK

1 recipe Sambusak Pastry (see p. 82)

for the filling:

2 tbsp olive oil

1 large onion, sliced

½ pound (200g) peeled and cooked potatoes

1 tsp za'atar or dried thyme

4 ounces (100g) halloumi or mozzarella, drained and grated

4 ounces (100g) feta cheese, crumbled

salt and freshly ground black pepper, to taste

1 egg, beaten

black onion (nigella) seeds and sesame seeds, to finish

flour or oil, for rolling the dough

Start by preparing and resting your dough (see p. 82). Preheat the oven to 375°F (190°C/170°C fan/gas 5).

To make the filling, pour the olive oil into a heavy-bottomed saucepan and heat gently. Add the onion with a splash of water and cook until the onion softens, then increase the heat and cook until the onion just starts to turn golden. Remove the pan from the heat, then add the potatoes and enough salt and pepper to intensify the flavor. Stir in the za'atar and set aside to cool. Once cool, stir in the cheeses.

Divide the dough into balls about ¾ to 1 inch (2 to 3cm) across — the exact size doesn't matter as you will save and reroll the trimmings. Set aside to rest, covered, on your work surface for about 15 minutes.

Roll out each dough ball on a lightly floured or oiled surface to about ¼ inch (½cm) thick. Place 1 to 2 teaspoons of the filling in the middle of each, then brush a little water around the edges. Fold the dough over, then press the edges down well so the filling is neatly secured. Take a teaspoon and scallop the edges slightly by cutting pieces away. Place on a baking sheet lined with parchment paper while you make the remainder.

Brush the tops of the sambusak with beaten egg, sprinkle with black onion and sesame seeds, and bake for 20 to 25 minutes until golden.

Lamb kibbeh FILLING

The traditional lamb filling for kibbeh should be kept light, so that when you bite through the denser, smooth texture of the fried crust you break through to a filling that's delicate with identifiable pieces of lamb, pine nut, and onion. I like to use a complex mixture of spices, but if you don't have them all available just add the ones that appeal to you most.

MAKES ENOUGH FILLING FOR 15 KIBBEH

for the baharat spice mix:

1½ tsp paprika

1 tsp freshly ground black pepper

1 tsp ground cumin

¾ tsp ground coriander

¾ tsp ground cinnamon

¾ tsp ground cloves

¾ tsp freshly grated nutmeg

¼ tsp ground cardamom

1 tbsp olive oil or butter

½ cup (75g) pine nuts

1 medium onion, finely chopped

¾ pound (300g) ground lamb

1 tsp salt

1 tbsp pomegranate molasses

In a small bowl, combine the baharat spice mix ingredients and set aside.

Heat the oil or butter — I prefer butter, as it gives a richer flavor — in a large, heavy-bottomed saucepan and fry the pine nuts gently until they begin to turn golden. Spoon the pine nuts onto a plate, leaving the oil in the pan, then add the onion and fry until soft and translucent. Add the lamb and salt, increase the heat, and fry until the moisture evaporates and the lamb begins to turn a rich brown.

Spoon the lamb into a mixing bowl, add the pine nuts, 2 teaspoons of the spice mix, and the molasses, stir well, then set aside to cool completely before using.

KIBBEH

Kibeh Lahma

This dish may appear curious at first. Essentially it's very lean and finely ground lamb, mixed with bulgur wheat, chopped onion and spices and wrapped around more lamb. To be utterly traditional and get the best results, you should grind the meat yourself, using the fine attachment on a grinder. I find that if I chop the meat as finely as I can, then place it in the food processor and pulse it a few times I can get a very good texture.

MAKES ABOUT 15 KIBBEH

1 ²/₃ cups (250g) fine bulgur wheat, soaked in tepid water for 30 to 60 minutes until soft

1 pound (500g) lean lamb, finely ground

1 small onion, very finely chopped (if possible, grind it further in a food processor)

1 tsp ground allspice

1 tsp Lebanese 7-spice mix

1 tsp freshly ground black pepper

½ tsp ground cinnamon

1 tsp salt

2 to 3 tbsp ice-cold water

1 recipe Lamb Kibbeh Filling (see p. 92)

vegetable oil, for frying

Drain the bulgur well. Tip it into the center of a clean kitchen towel, fold the towel over it, and rub it well so the bulgur breaks up slightly. Then chill for 30 minutes so the bulgur also dries slightly.

Put the meat through a grinder twice, using the fine attachment, or pulse it a few times in a food processor. Put the meat in a bowl, add the chilled bulgur wheat and the onion, and work everything together. Add the spices and salt, then work the mixture again, really squeezing and kneading the meat until it starts to hold together very well, adding the ice-cold water to give a soft, malleable consistency.

To shape the kibbeh for frying, wet your hands and take a large spoonful of the mixture. Place this in the palm of one hand, press into it with the thumb of the other to make a deep indentation, then use the thumb to press it to an even thickness. Spoon some of the Lamb Kibbeh Filling inside, then close the meat around the filling, using fingers dampened with a little water to smooth the seam and trap the filling inside. Squeeze the ends of the dough so they form points. Cover and chill for at least 1 hour.

To fry, pour 1 to 1½ inches (3 to 4cm) of oil (or enough to allow the kibbeh to fry without touching the bottom) into a heavy-bottomed saucepan. Heat the oil to about 350°F (180°C), or until a small piece of the meat mixture browns in about 2 minutes. Place a few of the kibbeh in the oil at a time, fry for 2 to 3 minutes or until brown and crisp, then remove with a slotted spoon. Test the center of the first one to check that it's piping hot, then allow to drain on paper towels while you fry the remainder.

PUMPKIN kibbeh

Kibeh Lakteen

Though making kibbeh with a pumpkin crust sounds very New World, it's utterly traditional. I use a lamb filling (see p. 92) with the pumpkin kibbeh but replace the pine nuts with roughly chopped walnuts and serve them with a little pomegranate molasses and sesame seeds on the top.

MAKES ABOUT 15 KIBBEH

1 recipe Lamb Kibbeh Filling (see p. 92)

¾ pound (300g) peeled pumpkin or butternut squash, deseeded and cut into chunks

1 ⅓ cups (200g) bulgur wheat, soaked for 30 to 60 minutes in tepid water until barely soft

all-purpose flour

1 tsp salt

1 tsp allspice

1 tsp cumin

Drain the bulgur well. Tip it into the center of a clean kitchen towel, fold the towel over it, and rub it well so the bulgur breaks up slightly. Then chill for 30 minutes wrapped in the towel so the bulgur also dries slightly.

Place the pumpkin or squash in a saucepan, cover with water, bring to a boil, then simmer until barely tender, 10 to 20 minutes, depending on the type of pumpkin or squash you're using. Drain and mash well, then mix with the bulgur and let stand for an hour so the bulgur absorbs the moisture from the pumpkin.

Add the salt and spices, mix well, then add enough flour to make a soft dough that holds its shape. Following the method for the Lamb Kibbeh recipe (see p. 94), fill, shape, and fry the kibbeh.

FALAFEL

These falafel can be made and fried in advance and then reheated in the oven before serving. I've even frozen them once fried and cooled, then reheated them from frozen. Place them on a baking sheet in a cold oven, switch it on to 400°F (200°C/180°C fan/gas 6), and cook the falafel for 25 minutes. It's essential that all the ingredients are completely dry to avoid the falafel falling apart, and make sure that the chickpeas and beans are well soaked but not fully cooked. Also, the starch in the fava beans does a better job of holding the mixture together, so you may have trouble if you just use chickpeas. Test one in the oil first, and if it breaks apart, just stir in a little chickpea flour to help it hold together.

MAKES ABOUT 20 BALLS

for the falafel spice mix:

2 tsp ground coriander

1 tsp ground cumin

¼ tsp ground caraway

1 tsp salt

3 cups (500g) chickpeas, soaked overnight and drained

1 ⅓ cups (200g) split fava beans, soaked overnight and drained

3 spring onions, finely chopped

1 celery stalk

3 garlic cloves, peeled and mashed

1 small bunch flat-leaf parsley, chopped

1 large bunch cilantro, chopped

1 tsp baking soda

3 tbsp sesame seeds

1 fresh green chile, chopped (optional)

grapeseed or sunflower oil, for frying

To make the spice mix, combine the ingredients in a small bowl and set aside.

Dry the soaked chickpeas and beans on a clean cloth to remove any moisture, then place in the bowl of a food processor with the spring onions, celery, garlic, and the spice mix. If your food processor bowl is small you may want to do this in batches. Process it as evenly as you can, so that the mixture looks very finely minced rather than puréed. Pat the herbs dry before chopping and adding to the bowl with the baking soda, sesame seeds, and chile, if using. Leave the mixture to sit for 15 minutes then take ¼ cup (40g) spoonfuls of the mixture and squeeze these tightly in your hands to form balls for deep-frying, or flatter discs for shallow-frying.

TO DEEP-FRY

Heat oil in a deep-fat fryer to 350°F (170°C). Test one ball to check that it doesn't fall apart, then fry the falafel in batches for 2 to 3 minutes until they turn a dark nut brown on the outside. Cut one open to check it's cooked through: if it's not, return it to the oil and fry for longer or place on a baking sheet in a hot oven for a few minutes to bake.

TO SHALLOW-FRY

Pour enough oil into a heavy-bottomed frying pan to cover the base. Pat the falafel into discs about ½ inch (1cm) thick and fry them in batches for 2 minutes each side, adjusting the heat so that they're crisp and brown.

FALAFEL

Spiced Fried POTATOES

Batata Harra

In this mezze dish, hot crisp cubes of potato are dressed with lemon and fresh cilantro and sometimes spiced, depending on what I'm serving them with. Parboiling the potato cubes avoids you having to fry them for so long. At home I shallow-fry these but at Comptoir we deep-fry them.

SERVES 4

2 pounds (1kg) potatoes, peeled and cut into 1-inch (2cm) dice

2/3 cup (150ml) olive or sunflower oil

3 garlic cloves, sliced

salt, to taste

handful of cilantro leaves

juice of 1 lemon

2 tsp ground cumin, optional

1/2 tsp paprika, optional

Parboil the potatoes in boiling salted water for no more than 3 minutes. Drain the potatoes. Heat the oil in a frying pan. When the oil is hot, add the potatoes and fry until golden, adding the garlic 2 to 3 minutes before the potatoes are done so it cooks.

Once the potatoes are crispy, drain the oil from the pan. Season the potatoes with salt, then mix with the cilantro, spoon it onto a plate, and squeeze the lemon juice over.

If you want to add more spices, return the potatoes to the pan once you've drained the oil away, sprinkle the cumin and paprika over evenly, season, and toss over high heat for 1 minute before serving with the cilantro and lemon.

SPICED
FRIED *POTATOES*

Batata Harra

ch 4. *Mezze* Hot Dishes

Mezze Hot Dishes

Mezze is all about presenting lots of different ingredients, flavors, and textures, so naturally it's also good to mix up hot and cold. This mix is utterly typical of Lebanese mezze. The dishes in this chapter will allow you to extend the range and breadth of the dishes you're serving and offer your guests something a little more substantial as well.

Many of these dishes work on their own. The Pomegranate Sautéed Chicken Livers (see p. 112) are quick and easy to prepare and would make an easy midweek supper on their own, as would the rich, soothing Moussaka (see p. 124), which is perfect for impressing your friends. If you wanted to add more hot alternatives to a mezze selection, turn to the Grills & Barbecues chapter (see p. 128) for some simple grilled meats, such as Chicken Wings (see p. 138) or Cinnamon-Marinated Quail (see p. 146).

Almond-crusted *squid with* sumac MAYONNAISE

This dish was inspired by a chef friend's restaurant in Beirut. The almond forms an utterly delicious crisp crust on the outside of the squid. Sumac, a crushed dried red berry, has a sour astringent flavor a little like lemon, so mixing it into a simple mayonnaise complements the lemon juice and brings out the citrus element.

SERVES 6 TO 8

1½ pounds (750g) squid, either just the tubes or with tentacles as well

scant ½ cup (100ml) plain yogurt

for the coating:

1¼ cups (150g) all-purpose flour

2 eggs, beaten

1 cup (100g) ground almonds

1 cup (100g) dried bread crumbs

for the sumac mayonnaise:

⅔ cup (150g) store-bought mayonnaise

2 tbsp labneh (see p. 58) or plain yogurt

1 tsp ground sumac

1 tbsp fresh lemon juice

grapeseed or rapeseed oil, for deep-frying

Wash the squid, then pat dry with paper towels. Cut the tubes into rings and the tentacles (if you're using them) into 1½ to 2-inch (4- to 5cm) pieces, and place in a bowl. Mix in the yogurt and chill for 2 to 3 hours. The yogurt marinade makes the squid more tender.

When you're ready to prepare your squid, place the flour in a shallow bowl, place the beaten eggs in another bowl, and the almonds and bread crumbs in a third. I also have a sink filled with warm soapy water ready to wash my hands in as this part is a bit messy. Line a large baking sheet with parchment paper. Drain the squid, toss a few pieces in the flour mixture, then dip them in the egg, and finally toss them in the almond bread crumbs before placing the coated squid on the lined baking sheet. Repeat with the remaining squid, then set in the fridge to chill while you get the oil ready and prepare the mayonnaise.

Beat the mayonnaise, labneh, sumac, and lemon juice together in a small bowl and set aside until ready to serve.

Heat enough oil for deep-frying in a deep, heavy-bottomed pan or deep-fat fryer to about 350°F (175°C). Check that the oil is hot enough by frying a piece of the coated squid: it should turn golden brown in about a minute. Fry the squid in batches, making sure there's enough room to avoid the pieces touching too much. When they're golden, remove with a slotted spoon and drain on paper towels while you fry the rest.

Serve the squid with the sumac mayonnaise alongside.

POMEGRANATE sautéed CHICKEN *livers*

Qasbatt dajaj

There are lots of ways to cook and serve chicken livers in Lebanon, and this one uses pomegranate molasses, which tastes like extra-tart cranberry juice that has been simmered until only a syrup remains. Imagine that intensity and that's what you get with pomegranate molasses. I've tried using a reduction of sharp cranberry juice as a substitute and it tastes brilliant, but you should be able to find the real thing if you look. As this is a mezze dish, it's not traditional to have rice on the side. Serve it with a layer of hummus underneath and in my view, you have the perfect treat.

SERVES 4 TO 6

1 pound (450g) chicken livers
3 tbsp olive oil
1 garlic clove, chopped
juice of 1 lemon
½ tsp ground cinnamon
pomegranate molasses, to taste
salt and freshly ground black pepper, to taste

serving suggestions:
chopped mint leaves
fresh pomegranate seeds
Crispy Onions (see p. 158)
Hummus (see p. 72)

Clean the livers, pat them dry with paper towels, and then trim off any membrane. Put the olive oil into a large, heavy-bottomed frying pan, get it moderately hot but not smoking, then add the garlic and stir well. As soon as the garlic slightly colors, add the livers to the pan in a single layer, with a little space between them; if your pan is small, cook them in batches (with more oil and garlic).

Increase the heat and leave the livers undisturbed for a minute or so until they just begin to color underneath. Then flip them over and cook the other side. When they begin to firm slightly but are still a little pink, add the lemon juice, salt and pepper to taste, and the cinnamon. Stir well, then pour on enough pomegranate molasses to coat the livers. Simmer gently until the livers are cooked, then serve.

You could try any of the serving suggestions: a hefty sprinkling of fresh mint and pomegranate seeds over the top is good, or a generous topping of crispy, fried onions. But one of my favorite ways is to spoon the hot livers onto a pile of hummus. The hummus gets warmed by the hot livers and they taste spectacular together.

Potato fritter
FILLED *with spiced* LAMB

Kibeh Batata

These fritters are a little like a potato kibbeh, except I fry them in a flat pan so they end up like potato cakes, rather than smooth, rounded kibbeh. If ever you want an utterly comforting Sunday breakfast meal, try these. Boiling large potatoes whole takes a while (microwaving them is much faster) but it stops them taking on water that could cause your potato cakes to fall apart. The drier the cooked potato, the better the potato cake. The lamb I use is similar to the topping for the Man'ousha (see p. 212), and if you have some left over, you can freeze it to use later as a flatbread topping.

SERVES 4 TO 5

for the potato crust:

3 large potatoes, boiled in their skins until tender

½ cup (50g) all-purpose flour or potato flour, plus extra for shaping cakes

1 tsp salt

1 egg

for the lamb filling:

2 to 3 tbsp olive oil, plus 1 tbsp

1 onion, finely diced

2 tomatoes, finely chopped

2 garlic cloves, sliced

¾ pound (300g) ground lamb

2 tsp paprika

1 tbsp Lebanese 7-spice powder

toasted pine nuts (optional)

vegetable oil, for frying

salt and freshly ground black pepper, to taste

Peel the potatoes while they're hot and then mash them in a bowl with the flour. Add the salt, mash well again, then do the same with the egg. Set aside until completely cool before using.

For the filling, pour 2 to 3 tablespoons of oil into a frying pan, add the onion with a splash of water, and cook until the onion is translucent and soft. Add the tomatoes and garlic, then cook until the moisture has evaporated and the mixture is starting to sizzle. Spoon this into a bowl, add the remaining tablespoon oil to the pan along with the lamb, and cook over high heat until the lamb is browned and dry. Add the tomato mixture and the spices, and season with salt and pepper. If you like, you can add toasted pine nuts as well. Heat again until the mixture is sizzling, then set aside to cool completely before using.

Make the fritters whatever size you like. Take a ball of cooled, cooked potato in a floured hand and make a depression in the center. Spoon some cold ground lamb into the center and then pinch the potato around it to trap the filling inside. On a lightly floured work surface, pat the cake flat and shape the sides neatly. Repeat with the remaining potato and lamb mixtures.

You can either fry or bake the potato cakes. To fry, heat a drizzle of vegetable oil in a frying pan over medium heat. Fry the cakes in batches, until golden brown on each side, then place in a low oven to keep warm while you fry the remainder.

ZUCCHINI *fritters*

Pale squashes similar to zucchini are often used in Lebanese cooking, and are typically stuffed and braised. These fritters have probably been influenced by Turkish cooking somewhere in time, perhaps even going back to the Ottoman empire, but for me they reflect simple home cooking at its best. I prefer to cook them as small freeform pieces in deep oil, though you can shallow-fry them patted out flat with a spoon. They are absolutely delicious served hot with Labneh with Black Olives and Mint (see p. 56) and a squeeze of lemon juice.

MAKES AT LEAST 15

5 zucchini

1 tsp salt

2 onions

2 to 3 tbsp olive oil

5 ounces (150g) feta

3 eggs, beaten

small bunch of mint, leaves only, chopped into shreds

freshly ground black pepper, to taste

½ tsp baking powder

all-purpose flour, for the batter

vegetable oil, for deep-frying

Grate the zucchini into a bowl, then sprinkle on the salt and set aside for 30 minutes.

Squeeze handfuls of the grated zucchini until they release as much liquid as possible, then place the dry zucchini to one side, discard the liquid, and return the zucchini to the bowl.

Grate the onions. Heat the olive oil in a heavy-bottomed frying pan over medium heat, then fry the onions until soft. Add the onions to the bowl with the zucchini and stir well. Crumble in the feta and add the beaten eggs.

Add the mint and plenty of pepper. Stir everything together, then add the baking powder and enough flour to make a soft batter (you can always adjust the consistency later).

Heat 1 to 1½ inches (2 to 3cm) of vegetable oil in a deep, heavy-bottomed saucepan. When you think it is hot, test the temperature with some of the batter. It should fry to a golden brown in 2 minutes, so lower the heat and allow the oil to cool if it colors too quickly. Spoon rounded tablespoons of batter into the oil in batches and fry until golden. Drain on paper towels, test the first ones to check that they're cooked in the middle, then keep warm in a low oven while you fry the remainder.

SESAME- and- black-seed-crusted *goat's cheese* with **MINT**

Though you could use pieces of halloumi cheese here, I find that goat's cheese gives a tangier and more refreshing result, as well as the satisfaction of it breaking through the sesame crust and having the molten cheese run out onto the plate.

SERVES 6

1¼ cups (150g) all-purpose flour

1 tbsp dried thyme or za'atar

1 tsp salt, plus a pinch

2 eggs

about 1 cup (100g) dried bread crumbs, finely ground

about ⅓ cup (50g) black onion (nigella) seeds

about ⅓ cup (50g) sesame seeds

6 small, firm goat's cheeses (crottins de chèvre) or slices cut from a large round

vegetable oil, for deep-frying

½ cucumber, cut into thin strips

bunch of mint, leaves only

handful of toasted walnuts or pistachios

First, prepare the dishes to coat the cheese: have 3 bowls ready, and somewhere to wash your hands, as it can get a bit messy. In one bowl toss together the flour, thyme, and 1 teaspoon of the salt. In another bowl, beat the eggs with a pinch of the salt. Finally, in the last bowl, mix together the bread crumbs and the seeds.

Trim the cheeses free of rind, then coat them in the spiced flour, dip into the egg to coat completely, and then roll them in the crumb-and-seed mix until covered evenly.

Heat some oil in a deep, heavy-bottomed saucepan, not filling it more than a third full so the oil can bubble up safely. Take the temperature to about 350°F (175°C) or test it with a cube of bread: you want it to turn golden brown in about 2 minutes. Fry the cheeses in batches, making sure there's enough oil around each so they fry evenly. When they're golden brown, scoop them out of the oil with a slotted spoon onto some paper towels while you fry the remainder.

Serve hot or warm on a bed of cucumber strips scattered with mint leaves and toasted walnuts or pistachios.

Moussaka *with* TAHINI

Moussaka bil Tahina

In the UK, moussaka is most commonly served in its Greek form, as a predominantly eggplant-and-meat-based baked dish topped with a rich béchamel sauce. But in fact the dish crops up in several national cuisines. There are Turkish, Serbian, and Egyptian versions, as well as this traditional Levantine recipe, which is often served as a mezze dish, either hot or cold.

This version is purely vegetarian and is lighter than its Greek counterpart as the key flavor is an intense tomato sauce. Don't skip the tahini dressing — the flavor of the sesame seeds and the cooling yogurt are a fabulous contrast to the dish itself and round it out perfectly.

SERVES 4

2 eggplants

salt

2 tbsp olive oil, plus extra for brushing and drizzling

1 large onion, finely chopped

4 garlic cloves, crushed

2¼ cups (400g) chopped tomatoes

1 tbsp tomato paste

6 tomatoes, sliced

1 (14-ounce/400g) can chickpeas, drained

freshly ground black pepper

for the tahini dressing:

½ cup (125g) yogurt

3 tbsp (40g) tahini

couple of pinches of za'atar

flat-leaf parsley, chopped

Take one eggplant and chop it into bite-size cubes, lay them on a plate, and cover with salt. Set aside for 15 minutes to draw out all the bitter juices. Slice the other eggplant into rounds, then salt them and set aside. Heat 1 tablespoon of the oil in a large pan and sauté the onion for 10 to 15 minutes, until it's starting to soften and caramelize.

Rinse the cubed eggplant and add it to the pan with the remaining tablespoon of oil. Cook, stirring from time to time, for about 10 minutes, until the eggplant cubes have softened and turned golden.

Stir in the garlic and cook in the heat of the pan for a couple of minutes until you can smell the aroma. Pour in the chopped tomatoes and tomato paste and bring everything to a simmer. Cover and cook over the lowest heat for 15 minutes.

Preheat the broiler and oil a baking sheet. Rinse the salt from the eggplant slices and brush them liberally with oil. Broil the slices until golden, turning them halfway through.

Preheat the oven to 400°F (200°C/180°C fan/gas 6).

Place a layer of the eggplant sauce in the bottom of an ovenproof dish, then cover this with the sliced tomatoes, chickpeas, and finally the broiled eggplant. Drizzle with a little extra oil and season with pepper. Bake for 20 minutes, until bubbling and golden on top.

To make the dressing, stir together the yogurt, tahini, and za'atar to taste. Scatter the chopped parsley over the moussaka and serve with the tahini dressing.

Grilled EGGPLANT WITH FETA

This isn't really a traditional dish as such, but it takes typical flavors and ingredients from the region and pairs them in what can only be described as a very addictive way. The saltiness of the feta works beautifully against the soft, simple flavor of the eggplant. You get crunch from the pine nuts, freshness from the mint, and just a hint of spice from the za'atar.

SERVES 4

olive oil

1 eggplant

salt and freshly ground black pepper, to taste

4 ounces (100g) feta

1 garlic clove, finely chopped

2 tbsp (25g) pine nuts

small handful of mint, shredded, plus a few extra leaves

za'atar, to finish

Preheat the broiler to hot. Lightly oil a baking sheet.

Lay the eggplant on a cutting board and trim the stalk off the end. Slice the eggplant lengthwise into thin slices. Brush generously with oil, season with salt and pepper, and lay the slices on the prepared baking sheet.

Broil until golden, then turn the slices and broil the other side.

Put the feta in a bowl and use a fork to crumble the cheese into small pieces. Add a drizzle of oil and the garlic, then mix again. Stir in the pine nuts.

Spoon the feta mixture evenly over the eggplant, then pop under the broiler again for a minute or two, just to warm the feta.

Place on a serving platter, then scatter the shredded mint leaves and za'atar over the top, and serve.

ch 5. *Grills* **&** Barbecues

Grills & Barbecues

Cooking over a grill or barbecue is very common in Lebanese and Arabic households, and in fact one of the Arab world's finest examples of a grilled meat preparation, the shawarma, is also one of its most famous culinary exports. Sadly, what is a flavorsome and succulent way of serving different types of meat in the Levant and Middle East has traveled badly, and the interpretations we encounter so often in the U.S. and UK bear little resemblance to the original.

As a means of keeping life simple, grilling really does tick all the boxes for me. An interesting marinade and a griddle pan or some hot coals are all you need to pack your meat or fish full of fabulous flavor, all finished off with that lovely charcoal backnote. And depending on the size of your chosen meat, it can be a really quick and easy method of cooking.

The dishes in this chapter could all be presented as part of a mezze selection; they could be served up together to create a sort of "mixed grill," and I've also given some suggestions for turning some of them into a main course for an easy midweek meal.

Pan-fried SHAWARMA

Shawarma

Shawarma is an Arabic meat preparation in which layers of meat are stacked on a large rotating spit and broiled. The meat is then shaved off in slices and served most commonly in bread with any number of accompaniments, including hummus, tahini, tabbouleh, and pickled turnips.

This recipe is my attempt at recreating the essence of the shawarma in a home kitchen. Skewers hold stacks of sliced meat together, creating a wide block of meat that you can crisp in a frying pan without drying the meat. You can then fry the spiced onions and remaining marinade from the meat and serve them with the lamb. Or you can put the skewered shawarma slabs under the broiler if that's easier.

SERVES 4

1¾ pounds (800g) leg or shoulder of lamb, off the bone

scant ¼ cup (50ml) cider vinegar

scant ¼ cup (50ml) fresh lemon juice

1½ tsp salt

1 garlic clove, crushed

2 onions, finely sliced

scant ¼ cup (50ml) olive oil

2 tbsp labneh (see p. 56) or thick yogurt

1 tbsp shawarma spice mix or Falafel Spice Mix (see p. 98)

8 thin bamboo skewers

Cut the lamb into 1 inch- (3cm-) wide strips, ideally about 4 inches (10cm) long. In a mixing bowl, stir the vinegar and lemon juice with the salt and garlic, then mix in the onions, oil, labneh, and spices. Add the lamb, stir well, then cover and leave to marinate for at least 4 hours so the acidity starts to tenderize the lamb and helps the spices to be absorbed.

Take a couple of sheets of aluminum foil, about 12 inches (30cm) square, and lay a block of strips of lamb in the center of it so they sit about 1 inch (3cm) high and about 4 inches (10cm) square. It's a little tricky, as you have to have the strips of meat standing on edge and they're all different sizes. But the foil helps to hold everything in place. Then fold the foil up and over firmly each way so the meat is held in place, and leave on a plate for another hour, or overnight, to firm up.

To cook, get your frying pan very hot. Carefully push the skewers vertically through the foil so the meat is secured, then trim the ends off with scissors. Tear the foil back, drop the shawarma slab into the frying pan, and fry until very brown underneath before flipping. If the meat needs to be cooked for longer, move it to a rimmed baking sheet and bake at 400°F (200°C/180°C fan/gas 6) for 5 to 10 minutes.

To serve, transfer to a cutting board and slice through the strips of meat with a sharp knife.

LAMB & pistachio *kofta*

In Arabic kofta means meatball, though in Arabic cuisine meatballs are not always round and are just as often shaped into "torpedoes," patties, or long sausages. They can be cooked in a sauce (see p. 168), or left plain and simply broiled or pan-fried as they are here. The secret to how good your koftas taste depends on how you flavor them. The meat is lean and needs plenty of salt and pepper, together with herbs and/or spices. In this version of the kofta, which we serve at Comptoir, we also throw in a handful of chopped pistachios, which add a bit of crunch. I would serve these very simply with tabbouleh (see p. 24), a drizzle of garlic sauce (see p. 228), and flatbreads.

SERVES 4 TO 6

1 pound (500g) lean ground lamb or beef

1 small onion, grated

⅔ cup (150g) pistachios, roughly chopped

2 tbsp chopped flat-leaf parsley

1 red chile, deseeded and chopped

1 tsp ground cumin

1 tsp ground coriander

¼ tsp ground allspice

salt and freshly ground black pepper, to taste

olive oil, for frying

Put the ground lamb in a bowl and add the onion, pistachios, parsley, chile, and spices. Season well with salt and pepper and use your hands to mix everything together thoroughly.

Scoop up 2-teaspoon portions of the mixture and form into small log shapes, squeezing the mixture to mold them. Flatten each side slightly on a board to give them a boxy shape.

Heat a griddle pan until hot. Brush a little olive oil over the koftas and fry in batches of 5 or 6 for about 2 minutes on each side. Cut through one to check there are no pink bits left in the meat, and they're ready.

CHICKEN wings

Jawaneh

Chicken wings that have been very simply marinated in lemon juice and garlic are a common mezze dish in Lebanon. The resulting flavors are fresh and zingy, but if you go one step further and add allspice to the marinade, this simple grilled dish can be lifted even higher.

SERVES 4 TO 6

juice of 1 lemon, plus 1 lemon, halved

2 tbsp olive oil, plus an extra drizzle

1 garlic clove, crushed

2 tsp chile paste (see p. 234)

½ tsp ground cinnamon

½ tsp ground cardamom

1 tsp ground allspice

salt, to taste

12 chicken wings

In a bowl, mix together the lemon juice, olive oil, garlic, chile paste, and spices, and season well with salt. Put the chicken wings in a large, non-metallic dish and spoon the marinade over them. Brush it all over the chicken to coat, then chill for at least 1 hour.

Take the chicken out of the fridge half an hour before you're going to cook it, to take the chill off it. Heat a large, heavy-bottomed frying pan until hot and add a drizzle of oil.

Fry the chicken wings in batches for 5 to 8 minutes on each side, taking care that the spices don't burn. Add the lemon halves to the pan and squeeze gently to extract the juice while cooking, to give the chicken extra flavor.

To see if they're cooked, push a knife into the thickest part of the wing and check that there are no pink bits or juices running out.

Comptoir **kofta** *hot dog*

The great thing about food is that there aren't any rules. At Comptoir I'd like to think that while we stick by tradition and authenticity for much of what we serve, we also have the freedom to experiment and twist things to make them even better or even more exciting. This dish is one of those times. I love the Lebanese kofta but I also love the American hot dog so here I've put the two together. The kofta, made with ground lamb, is seasoned with onion, fresh herbs, and coriander but still works well with classic hot dog accompaniments. We make our own buns, which are soft and slightly sweet, and I think they go brilliantly with these koftas, but if you're short on time then store-bought buns are fine. If you want to soften the flavor of the chopped onions slightly, blanch them in boiling water for a couple of minutes first, then allow to cool before mixing with the ground lamb.

SERVES 4

Crispy Onions (see p. 158)
1 pound (500g) ground lamb
1 small onion, finely chopped
2 tbsp chopped fresh thyme leaves
1 tbsp chopped fresh parsley
1 tsp ground coriander
1 tsp freshly ground black pepper
salt, to taste
olive oil, for frying
Tahini Butter Buns (see p. 204)
or hot dog rolls
tomato ketchup

First, prepare the crispy onions (see p. 158) and set aside.

Spoon the ground lamb into a bowl and add the chopped onion, thyme, parsley, coriander, and pepper, and season with salt. Use your hands to mix everything together, then divide the mixture into 4 even portions with a knife.

Lift out one portion and mold it with your hands to make a long sausage shape, roughly the same length as the buns you'll be using for serving. Do the same with the remaining portions of the lamb mixture so you end up with 4 sausage shapes.

Heat a large, heavy-bottomed frying pan until hot and add a drizzle of oil. Cook the hot dogs in batches for around 10 minutes until golden and cooked all the way through. Turn them every now and then so they are evenly colored.

Toast the sides of the buns on a griddle. Split them and push the koftas into the middle of each bun, drizzle with ketchup, scatter some crispy onions on top, and serve.

COMPTOIR
KOFTA **HOT DOG**

CINNAMON-
marinated QUAIL

Ferih

For such small birds, quail pack a lot of flavor, which is why they need little more than a simple marinade to accompany them. One quail per person makes for a starter or light supper, so this dish would be a good one to serve if you've prepared a generous mezze selection to start, as it won't be too heavy, particularly if combined with another light dish, such as the chicken wings on p. 138. If you wanted to serve it as a more substantial main course, you could either serve two quail per person, or bulk the dish out by serving it with rice (see p. 162) and a vegetable.

SERVES 4

4 quail

2 tbsp olive oil

1 tbsp honey

1 tsp ground cinnamon

1 tbsp pomegranate molasses

juice of ½ orange

salt and freshly ground black pepper, to taste

4 short cinnamon sticks (or 2 long ones, halved)

2 tsp sesame seeds

small handful of basil leaves, roughly torn

Put the quail on a board. Butterfly each quail by cutting down one side of the backbone. Open the bird out and use the heel of your hand to press down on the breast to flatten it. Do the same with the other 3 birds. Put in a large shallow dish.

Mix together 1 tablespoon of the oil with the honey, cinnamon, pomegranate molasses, and orange juice, and season well. Brush all over the quail and add the cinnamon sticks. Cover, chill, and marinate for 1 hour.

Take the quail out of the fridge about half an hour before cooking, to take the chill off them.

Heat a large, heavy-bottomed frying pan until hot and add the remaining 1 tablespoon of oil. Place the quail in the pan, skin-side down, and cook over medium heat for 8 to 10 minutes. Turn over and cook on the other side for a few more minutes. Add the sesame seeds and basil to the pan and stir to coat in the juices.

To see if the quail is cooked, use a skewer or knife to pierce the thickest part of the thigh and check that the juices run clear.

Chile-*marinated* JUMBO shrimp

You can buy chile paste in most supermarkets now and there are some very good ones available. Try making it fresh, though, and you can adjust the levels of seasoning and spice to suit your tastes. The best thing about this recipe for me is that by cooking the shrimp in their shells they retain plenty of flavor. I like to suck the juices out of the head after eating the shrimp. It may sound strange, but trust me, it's delicious!

SERVES 4

1 tbsp olive oil, plus extra for brushing

1 generous tbsp chile paste (store-bought, or homemade, see p. 234)

3 garlic cloves, crushed

1 tbsp chopped fresh parsley, plus extra to garnish

16 raw jumbo shrimp in their shells

salt and freshly ground black pepper, to taste

juice of ½ lemon

smoked paprika, for sprinkling

Mix together the oil, chile paste, garlic, and parsley in a large bowl. Add the shrimp, season well with salt and pepper, and toss to coat. Marinate in the fridge for 30 minutes.

Take the shrimp out of the fridge and thread them onto long metal skewers. Heat a griddle pan until hot, brush the shrimp with a little more oil and cook on the griddle for 2 to 3 minutes on each side, until the shrimp have all turned pink and opaque.

Place on a board or serving platter, squeeze over the lemon juice, sprinkle with paprika and parsley, and serve.

Pomegranate MOLASSES—
marinated SALMON

The secret to achieving a balance of flavors in this dish is in the amount of lemon juice you add. Salmon is quite a rich, oily fish and here it's partnered with syrupy pomegranate molasses — the two together risk being overwhelming and cloying. The acidic lemon juice is your tool for ensuring you cut through this richness, so after adding it make sure you taste the dish to check the balance is right before serving. The fresh pomegranate seeds provide color, of course, but the pop of the juice when you bite into them adds a delicious freshness to the dish.

SERVES 4

4 salmon fillets, about 5 ounces (150g) each

juice of 1 lemon, plus 1 lemon, halved

1 tbsp chopped fresh thyme leaves

salt and freshly ground black pepper, to taste

1 tbsp olive oil

1 tsp sumac

1 tbsp pomegranate molasses

seeds from ½ fresh pomegranate

small handful of mint leaves, chopped

Lay the salmon fillets on a plate or in a dish and drizzle the lemon juice over them. Sprinkle with the thyme, and season well with salt and pepper. Chill for 30 minutes to marinate.

Take the salmon out of the fridge. Heat a large, heavy-bottomed frying pan until hot and add the oil. Place the salmon in the pan, skin-side down. Add the lemon halves at the same time, putting them in cut-side down.

Reduce the heat to medium and cook for 5 to 8 minutes, until the salmon skin is crispy and the fillets look as though they're almost cooked through. Turn them over and cook on the other side. Squeeze the juice out of the lemon halves and add the pomegranate molasses and sumac. Taste to check that the balance of sweet and sour is right.

Serve the salmon with a sprinkling of pomegranate seeds and a few chopped fresh mint leaves.

ch 6. *Tabkhat*

Tabkhat

Tabkhat is a somewhat catch-all term used to describe a homestyle form of cooking in Lebanon — it's predominantly about one-pot dishes, with a heavy emphasis on stews. The recipes in this chapter embrace and reflect that; it is all about simple, hearty, warming dishes that would commonly be cooked in homes throughout the Lebanon.

The cooking techniques required are all quite basic — you'll be braising or slow-cooking the dishes in the oven — which allows you to turn very few simple ingredients into flavorsome meals. The herbs, spices, and aromatics are given time to develop, thereby deepening and pervading the basis of the dish, whether it's meat, fish, or vegetables. And best of all, these dishes generally *provide a wholesome, delicious, and nourishing meal in a single pot. You'll also find the widespread Middle Eastern accompaniment, the Lebanese method of cooking rice. I've no doubt you are familiar, if not with this, then perhaps with Indian or Asian pilaf. The Lebanese version keeps the dish very simple, mixing a little vermicelli pasta cooked in butter with the rice to add a different texture.* ●

Spiced *BAKED fish*

Samke harra

Though the whole fish look impressive here, the flavors work equally well with fillets, and the marinade gives a fresh, complex flavor. In Lebanon, this dish is called samke harra, and I'm told it originates in the city of Tripoli. At Comptoir, we serve this dish whenever we want the meal to feel like a mighty celebration. It can be served two ways: you can either bake the fish simply with a little lemon juice and serve it with the marinade on the side, or cook it all together.

SERVES 6

for the marinade:

2 onions, finely chopped

5 tbsp olive oil, plus extra for thinning the marinade

good pinch of salt

2 bell peppers (1 red and 1 green), deseeded and finely chopped

2 garlic cloves, finely chopped

1 tsp ground cumin

1 tsp ground coriander

2 small chiles (not too hot)

small bunch flat-leaf parsley, finely chopped

small bunch cilantro, finely chopped

juice of 1 lemon

1 cup (100g) walnuts or pine nuts, chopped (optional)

6 large fillets of sea bass, sea bream, or snapper, or 3 whole fish, scaled and cleaned with heads on

olive oil, for the baking dish

lemon slices

salt and freshly ground black pepper, to taste

Preheat the oven to 400°F (200°C/180°C fan/gas 6).

For the marinade, place the onions in a heavy-bottomed saucepan with the oil, salt, and a splash of water, then cook over high heat until the onions are translucent and dry. Add the bell peppers and cook until almost soft, then add the garlic and cook for a few more minutes, until tender. Add the spices and chiles, cook for 1 minute longer, then remove from the heat and spoon into a bowl. Stir in the parsley and cilantro, then add the lemon juice, walnuts or pine nuts, and enough extra oil to make a soft, spreadable marinade. Once cool, it will keep well in the fridge for a few days.

To bake the fish, lay the fillets in an oiled baking dish, or in a couple of larger ovenproof dishes if using whole fish, with slices of lemon either placed across the base of the dish or tucked inside the cavity of the fish. Spoon the marinade over and around the fish, then season with salt and pepper and bake in the oven until the fish is just cooked, 8 to 10 minutes for fillets and 18 to 20 minutes for whole fish. This is especially good served with tahini sauce and hot boiled rice.

Fried eggplant WITH yogurt, crispy onions, and toasted PITA

Fatet Batenjan

This dish is the perfect example of how mixing opposing flavors and sensations in a dish can create something wonderful. Piping-hot crispy onions and crunchy pita pieces are set against a gentle background of tender eggplant and a creamy yogurt and tahini sauce. The whole thing is finished with the freshness and sweetness of cool pomegranate seeds, which pop in your mouth and create a whole new level of sensation. Try it — I guarantee you'll be amazed.

SERVES 4

for the crispy onions:

1 cup (250ml) vegetable oil

1 large onion, finely sliced

salt and freshly ground black pepper, to taste

2 eggplants, cut into 1½-inch (4cm) pieces

salt

4 tbsp olive oil

2 pita breads, toasted until crisp and then broken into small pieces

1¼ cups (300g) plain yogurt

2 to 3 tbsp tahini

1 garlic clove, crushed

squeeze of lemon juice

freshly ground black pepper, to taste

1 tsp chile paste

seeds from ½ pomegranate

To make the crispy onions, pour the vegetable oil into a small, heavy-bottomed pan and place it over medium heat. Pat the sliced onion dry, then as soon as the oil is hot enough — it will sizzle when you drop a piece of onion into it — fry all of the onion until crisp and golden; this should take a couple of minutes. Lift out with a slotted spoon and drain on paper towels. Season well.

Spread the eggplant pieces out on a tray and sprinkle with salt. Set aside for 20 minutes to allow the salt to extract the bitter juices.

Tip the eggplant into a colander and rinse well to remove the salt and juices. Heat ¼ cup of the olive oil in a large frying pan and fry the eggplant in batches until the pieces are golden. Remove and set aside on a plate. Add the pita to the pan and fry briefly in any leftover oil to crisp and heat through.

In a separate small pan, mix together the yogurt, tahini, garlic, and lemon juice. Season with salt and pepper and beat everything together — if it's too thick, add a splash or two of cold water. Place the pan over low heat and heat gently until just warm.

In a small bowl, stir together the remaining 3 tablespoons oil and the chile paste.

To serve, spoon all the eggplant onto a plate and top with the pita bread pieces. Drizzle with the tahini yogurt, scatter the pomegranate seeds and crispy onions on top, and finish with the chile-oil mixture.

Spiced **ground lamb** *with* tomato, zucchini & eggplant

Mahashi

Stuffing vegetables with meat, or wrapping meat in vegetables such as cabbage leaves, is a popular way of preparing them in Lebanon as it enables cooks to stretch what might be quite a small quantity of meat into a substantial meal. Here, a small amount of ground lamb is turned into a hearty, generous dish simply by bulking it out with rice and adding a rich tomato sauce. Try to find the pale green zucchinis for this recipe. The ones that have a generous rounded end will be easier to fill with the ground lamb mixture.

SERVES 4

for the sauce:

2 tbsp olive oil

1 small onion, very finely chopped

1 garlic clove, crushed

2 (14-ounce/400g) cans chopped tomatoes

2½ cups (600ml) hot lamb stock

½ tsp dried mint

salt and freshly ground black pepper, to taste

for the stuffed vegetables:

4 long, thin eggplants

2 zucchini

¼ cup (50g) risotto rice, such as arborio

3 ounces (75g) ground lamb

1½ tbsp (20g) butter, melted

1 tsp ground allspice

handful of roughly chopped flat-leaf parsley, to serve

First, prepare the sauce. Heat the oil in a large, ovenproof casserole dish. (It needs to be large enough for the stuffed vegetables to sit in the sauce in a single layer.) Add the chopped onion, season well, and sauté, covered with a lid, for 10 to 15 minutes, until it starts to soften. Stir in the garlic and cook for 1 minute more.

Tip the chopped tomatoes into a food processor and whiz to chop the pieces a little more finely, then add to the onions. Add 1¾ cups (400ml) of the stock, along with the mint, and season again. Cover, then bring to a boil, and simmer over low heat for 30 minutes, checking the water level every now and then to make sure it doesn't get too low.

Preheat the oven to 400°F (200°C/180°C fan/gas 6). Trim the ends from the eggplants and carefully use a knife and small spoon to remove the seeds from the middle. Do the same with the zucchini, then set aside while you prepare the filling.

Wash the rice well and put it in a bowl with the ground lamb, melted butter, and allspice. Season the mixture and use your hands to mix all the ingredients together. Divide the mixture evenly between the holes in the eggplant and zucchini shells, leaving a small gap at either end for the filling to expand. Sit each piece in the sauce in the casserole dish, cover, and bake for 1 hour. After 30 minutes, turn the vegetables over and pour in the remaining ¾ cup (200ml) stock. When the vegetables are tender, sprinkle with the parsley and serve.

RICE *with* **vermicelli**

There are countless versions of this rice-based dish found across the Middle East and Asia, but while additional grains and ingredients may be added, the essence and aims are universal — perfectly cooked, fluffy rice, where each grain remains separate.

At Comptoir we stick to the dish's humble origins and cook the rice very simply with one of its common Lebanese partners, vermicelli pasta, and a little butter. When cooking the vermicelli, make sure the heat is low enough so that the butter doesn't burn, and keep stirring so the pasta colors evenly.

SERVES 4

3 tbsp (50g) butter

1½ ounces (50g) vermicelli pasta, broken into pieces

1 cup (200g) basmati or long grain rice

2 cups (500ml) boiling chicken or vegetable stock

2 bay leaves

salt

Melt the butter in a heavy-bottomed pan over low to medium heat, then add the pasta. Cook until golden brown, stirring continuously. Some of the pasta will start to color first — just keep stirring and it will soon all turn brown.

Stir in the rice, making sure it all gets well coated in the butter. Pour in the stock, add the bay leaves, and season well with salt. Cover with a lid and bring to a boil. Turn the heat down to its lowest setting and cook for 12 to 15 minutes until all the liquid has been absorbed. Turn off the heat and set aside for 5 minutes, then use a fork to fluff up the rice. Check the seasoning and serve.

TOMATO-CRUST potatoes

Think of this dish as a naked moussaka, with potatoes in place of the eggplant and not a single spoonful of béchamel in sight. The magic of the dish is its lightness and rich flavor, which is created using relatively few ingredients. Don't overcook it, as you want some texture in the potatoes — it's a hassle-free supper.

SERVES 6

4 tbsp olive oil

1 large onion, thickly sliced

good pinch of salt

2 garlic cloves, crushed

1½ pounds (750g) waxy potatoes, such as Yukon Gold or Red Bliss

2 pounds (1kg) large tomatoes, sliced

salt and freshly ground black pepper, to taste

1¼ cups (300ml) hot lamb or vegetable stock, plus a little extra

2 tsp dried thyme

½ tsp ground cinnamon

handful of mint leaves, roughly chopped

Preheat the oven to 400°F (200°C/180°C fan/gas 6). Heat 2 tablespoons of the oil in a heavy-bottomed pan, then sauté the onion with a good pinch of salt for 10 to 15 minutes until just soft and starting to turn golden. Stir in the garlic.

Peel the potatoes and slice into rounds about ¼ inch thick. Layer in an ovenproof dish with the sautéed onion and garlic, and slices of tomatoes, seasoning the ingredients well.

Drizzle the remaining oil over the vegetables and pour the hot stock over the top. Stir in the thyme and cinnamon, cover tightly with foil, and cook in the oven for 45 minutes. Uncover and continue to cook until the top is golden brown, 10 to 15 minutes. If it looks very dry, add a drizzle more stock. It's ready when the potatoes feel tender and a knife goes in easily.

Scatter the mint leaves over the top, and serve.

Meatballs

Daoud basha

There are literally hundreds of varieties of meatballs, not just in Lebanon, but across the whole of the Middle East, as well as parts of Asia. Simple, hearty, and incredibly adaptable on the flavor front, it's not hard to see why meatballs are so universally loved — to me, this is comfort food at its very best. Seasoning is the key here to ensure you have a well-flavored dish. To check, after seasoning the ground meat mixture, fry a little bit in a pan and taste to ensure the amount of salt, pepper, and spice is just right.

SERVES 4

for the sauce:

2 tbsp olive oil

3 onions, roughly chopped

½ eggplant, roughly chopped

1 zucchini, roughly chopped

1 garlic clove, crushed

1 green and 1 red bell pepper, deseeded and roughly chopped

1 cup (200g) chopped tomatoes

1 tbsp tomato paste

salt and freshly ground black pepper, to taste

3 cups (750ml) hot beef or lamb stock, plus a little extra

for the meatballs:

1 pound (500g) ground beef or lamb

1 small onion, finely grated

1½ tbsp (20g) pine nuts

½ tsp ground allspice

1 tsp Lebanese 7-spice mix

salt and freshly ground black pepper, to taste

2 to 3 tbsp olive oil

Rice (see p. 162), to serve

First, make the sauce. Heat the oil in a large, heavy-bottomed pan and sauté the onion for around 10 minutes until it starts to soften and caramelize. Add the eggplant and zucchini and continue to cook.

Stir in the garlic and cook for about 1 minute, until you can smell its aroma. Stir in the chopped bell peppers, tomatoes, and tomato paste, then season everything well and pour in the stock. Cover and bring to a boil, then leave to simmer over very low heat while you make the meatballs.

Put the ground meat in a large bowl and add the onion, spices, and plenty of seasoning. Roughly chop the pine nuts and add them to the bowl. Mix with your hands until all the ingredients are combined. Take lumps of the mixture, each about the size of an apricot, and roll into balls with your hands.

Heat the oil in a large, heavy-bottomed frying pan over medium heat. Add 4 or 5 meatballs at a time and gently fry until golden all over. Set aside on a plate while you cook the remaining meatballs.

Give the sauce, which has been gently simmering away, a good stir. You may need to add a little more stock or water at this stage if it's looking thick. Drop the meatballs on top, tucking them just under the liquid, and simmer for 25 to 30 minutes, or until the meatballs are tender, adding more stock if necessary. Serve with rice.

BRAISED *chicken* *with* beans

Loubiah bil dajaj

Allspice is one of the principal spices used in Lebanese cuisine. It is the dried fruit of the Pimenta Dioica tree and is believed to have been called allspice by the British, who thought it combined the flavors of cinnamon, cloves and nutmeg. It lends a warmth and earthy flavor to Lebanese food and is subtly able to lift dishes that might initially appear quite bland, as with this chicken stew.

Cooking the onions until they're slippery and soft is key here, so that the end result doesn't taste of raw onions. They need to get to the stage where they're just starting to caramelize to add more flavor to the stew. When adding the beans, make sure they're cooked for long enough — they should be tender and bendy, not squeaky and crisp.

SERVES 4

1 tbsp olive oil

1 onion, chopped

salt

4 skinless, boneless chicken breasts, cut into bite-size pieces

freshly ground black pepper, to taste

1 garlic clove, chopped

1 tbsp tomato paste

¼ tsp ground cinnamon

¼ tsp ground allspice

1 (14-ounce/400g) can chopped tomatoes

1¾ cups (450ml) hot chicken stock

2 cups (200g) green beans, trimmed and chopped

Heat the oil in a large, heavy-bottomed pan and sauté the onion with a little salt for 10 to 15 minutes, until softened and starting to caramelize.

Stir the chicken into the softened onions and cook until they start to turn golden. Season well.

Add the garlic, tomato paste, and spices, and mix everything together, then pour in the chopped tomatoes along with the stock. Almost cover the pan, so there's a little gap for some of the steam to escape, and allow the stew to gradually thicken, then bring up to a boil. Reduce the heat and simmer for 20 minutes.

Add the green beans to the pan and continue to cook for 5 to 8 minutes until the beans are cooked through but still have bite.

Fried sea *bass* with TAHINI *and* RICE

This is my version of sayadiah, a popular seafood dish in Lebanon and a good one for serving to large groups, as you can scale up the amount of fish fillets and rice as necessary. Sea bass has such a delicate flavor that you need to do very little to it — a very small amount of cumin is added here just to give it a hint of spice. The stronger flavors come from the rice element of the dish and all you need is a simple vegetable dish to serve alongside.

SERVES 4

3 tbsp tahini

1/3 cup (100g) plain yogurt

squeeze of lemon juice, plus lemon wedges to serve

salt and freshly ground black pepper, to taste

2 cups (500ml) hot fish stock

1¼ cups (250g) basmati rice

1 cup (250ml) vegetable oil

2 tbsp (25g) pine nuts

1 large onion, sliced

1 tbsp olive oil

½ tsp ground cumin

2 tbsp all-purpose flour

8 sea bass fillets, cut in half crosswise

flat-leaf parsley leaves, to garnish

Stir the tahini and yogurt together in a bowl. Season with the lemon juice and salt and black pepper, to taste. Set aside.

Put the fish stock into a small pan and bring to a boil. Add the rice and simmer on low heat according to the directions on the package.

Heat about 1 tablespoon of the vegetable oil in a heavy-bottomed saucepan and fry the pine nuts until golden. Remove with a slotted spoon and set aside. Pour the remaining vegetable oil into the pan and heat until a splash of water sizzles on contact with the oil.

Toss the onion into the hot oil and fry until golden. Lift out with a slotted spoon and drain on paper towels. Season with a pinch of salt.

Heat the olive oil in a separate large, heavy-bottomed frying pan. In a bowl, mix the cumin with the flour, then toss the fish in it. Fry the fish in batches, skin-side down, for a couple of minutes, then turn over and cook until just cooked through.

Fluff the rice with a fork and then spoon onto a large plate. Spoon the fish on top, then scatter the onion and pine nuts over the top. Drizzle with a little of the tahini sauce and serve the remainder in a bowl alongside. Garnish the dish with the parsley leaves and serve immediately with lemon wedges.

STUFFED *eggplant*

Batenjan mahshi

Eggplants are used abundantly in Middle Eastern cooking. They are available all year round and their ability to absorb other flavors readily lends itself well to this style of cooking.

Lebanese eggplants differ from the variety most commonly available in the US and UK. They are long and thin, which makes them well suited to being stuffed whole. If you can't get ahold of this variety, use six medium-size eggplants and cut them in half through the middle before pan-frying. They may take a little longer in the oven, so ease the end of one open with a knife and fork to check that it's cooked all the way through.

SERVES 6

2 tbsp olive oil

12 small, long eggplants

1 onion, finely chopped

1 garlic clove, finely chopped

1 pound (500g) ground lamb

½ tsp ground cinnamon

½ tsp ground allspice

3 tbsp (40g) pine nuts

⅔ cup (200ml) hot lamb stock

2 tbsp chopped fresh parsley

salt and freshly ground black pepper, to taste

to serve:

2 tbsp tahini (see p. 230)

Crispy Onions (see p. 158)

Preheat the oven to 375°F (190°C/170°C fan/gas 5). Heat 1 tablespoon of the olive oil in a large sauté pan and cook the eggplant, 2 or 3 at a time, until golden on each side. Lift out and put on a shallow roasting pan.

Heat the remaining 1 tablespoon of oil in the same pan and stir in the onion. Cook for around 15 minutes over low to medium heat until the onion has softened. Stir in the garlic, then the ground lamb and continue to cook until the lamb is browned all over.

Stir in the spices, pine nuts, and stock, and season well. Simmer, uncovered, for 15 to 20 minutes, until most of the liquid has been absorbed. Stir in the parsley.

Use a sharp knife to make a slit down the length of each eggplant, then gently ease each one apart. Season and spoon the lamb mixture into the gaps. Roast in the oven for 30 minutes.

While the eggplant is roasting, prepare the crispy onions. As soon as the eggplant has come out of the oven, drizzle the tahini over the top and sprinkle with the crispy onions.

Cumin-BRAISED neck of LAMB with BABY OKRA

Bamiah bil Lahma

Neck of lamb is a tough, fatty cut of meat that's sadly not a particularly popular cut in the US and UK. I'm probably not selling it to you but hopefully this dish might cause you to think again. When cooked slowly over several hours, lamb neck softens and becomes so beautifully tender, it almost falls off the bone. The bone also imparts so much rich flavor into the stew that you don't need many other ingredients to create a hearty meal. If you can't get hold of neck of lamb on the bone, use lamb crown chop, a meatier but slightly more expensive cut.

SERVES 4 TO 6

2 pounds (1kg) neck of lamb, bone-in, chopped into pieces

4 tbsp olive oil

1 tsp ground cumin

2 garlic cloves, chopped

1 onion, roughly chopped

2 carrots, roughly chopped

1 (14-ounce/400g) can chopped tomatoes

2½ cups (600ml) hot lamb stock

5 ounces (150g) okra, washed and roughly chopped

salt and freshly ground black pepper, to taste

chopped cilantro, to garnish

Spread the lamb out in a large dish. Mix together 2 tablespoons of the oil, the cumin, and the garlic and rub all over the pieces. Set aside to marinate for 30 minutes.

Heat a heavy-bottomed pan (or an ovenproof casserole, if you want to cook this in the oven later) over medium heat and fry the lamb neck in batches until golden on each side. Set aside on a plate.

Add the remaining oil to the pan and slide in the onion and carrots. Cook over medium heat for about 5 minutes, until the onion is starting to soften.

Pour in the tomatoes and lamb stock and return the lamb to the pan. Season well with salt and pepper, then cover and bring to a gentle boil. Turn the heat down to low and cook for about 1½ hours, checking the level of the liquid every now and then. Alternatively, if you would prefer to cook this in the oven, you could cook it in a preheated oven at 300°F (150°C/130°C fan/gas 3).

Place the okra on top of the stew, cover, and continue to cook for about 30 minutes, until tender. Check the seasoning, then serve, garnished with the cilantro.

ch 7. *Breakfast*

Breakfast

If you've never experienced a Middle Eastern breakfast, then you're in for a treat — and perhaps a surprise, too. For even at the breakfast table you're likely to be faced with the dilemma of how to try everything from the abundance of choice presented to you.

Breakfast, whether at home or in a café, will generally involve a plate of Labneh (see p. 56) or other soft cheeses, served with large quantities of flatbread, olive oil, tomatoes, and undoubtedly some Za'atar (see p. 186). You'll probably also find jams to accompany the breads.

Another very common breakfast dish is Ful Moudamas (see p. 194), a creamy broad bean dip, which may sound strange but is hugely popular and utterly delicious —

I'd really urge you to have a go at making your own, particularly to serve as part of a Full Lebanese Breakfast (see p. 190). And if eggs are your thing, then there are plenty of options on offer, too — omelettes, fried eggs with za'atar, scrambled, or even the Lebanese version of a Spanish tortilla.

Those with a sweeter tooth aren't neglected. The French influence on Lebanese history means that pastries such as croissants are a common sight, particularly the national adaptation — a za'atar croissant. A particularly sugary local option is knefeh — a soft cheese pastry, soaked in a sweet syrup and served wrapped in a thin sesame seed bread. Not one for the fainthearted! ●

FETA *and* *za'atar* omelette

Za'atar can cause a little confusion. It's the term for the Middle Eastern spice mix made from a heady combination of herbs, spices, and seeds; however, it's also the name of an herb itself. As with so much of Middle Eastern cooking, there are many regional variations. Its uses are limitless: it can be sprinkled over food on its own, stirred into dips or rice, or massaged over chicken or meat as a dry rub. In Lebanon, it's strongly associated with the breakfast table, where it's used in both a sweet and a savory context. Although there are some good ready-prepared versions available, nothing really compares to making your own — it's so easy to do and you can adjust the levels of each flavor according to your own preferences.

SERVES 2

2 large eggs

salt and freshly ground black pepper, to taste

1 tsp za'atar (store-bought, or homemade, see below)

1 tbsp olive oil, plus extra to serve

1 ounce (25g) feta cheese or firm goat's cheese, crumbled

Beat the eggs in a bowl and season well with salt and pepper and ½ teaspoon of the za'atar. Heat the oil in a heavy-bottomed frying pan, no bigger than 6½ to 7 inches (17 to 18cm) in diameter.

Pour in the beaten eggs and use a spatula to swirl the mixture around in the pan, drawing in parts of the omelette that have cooked and allowing the uncooked egg to run into the gaps. Continue to do this until all the egg is just set.

Scatter the cheese over the omelette and sprinkle the remaining za'atar over the top. Drizzle with extra oil, if you like, before serving.

Comptoir *Libanais* ZA'ATAR MIX

½ tsp sesame seeds

¼ tsp sumac

1 tsp dried thyme

1 tsp marjoram

1 tsp dried oregano

good pinch of sea salt

In a dry frying pan, toast the sesame seeds until just golden. Tip into a mortar and add the sumac and herbs with a good pinch of salt. Pound with the pestle until everything is well ground. Store in an airtight container and use within a month.

Full LEBANESE BREAKFAST

At Comptoir, my aim has always been to remain true to authentic Lebanese culture and cooking, while also being mindful of the fact that I'm running a restaurant that's in England and therefore I'm not necessarily catering to a Lebanese audience. Breakfast was quite a tricky meal to tackle, because each culture has its own very particular traditions and tastes. Could I convince the British to try the Lebanese equivalent of the Full English? The popularity of our "Full Lebanese" shows the willingness diners have to experience something new. This traditional Lebanese breakfast features crunchy falafel, hearty ful moudamas (a traditional broad bean dip), salty halloumi, creamy labneh, and while there are eggs in the form of fried eggs, they're spiced up with a sprinkling of sumac. It's easier if you prepare some of these elements ahead, so that you've got less to do on the day, but once they're in your fridge, this is a fabulously easy breakfast or brunch to throw together.

SERVES 4

Falafel (see p. 98)

Ful Moudamas (see p. 194)

1 tbsp olive oil, plus extra to serve

4 slices halloumi

4 large eggs

generous pinch of sumac

good pinch of sea salt

labneh (see p. 56)

za'atar (see p. 186 for homemade)

4 black olives, to garnish

chopped flat-leaf parsley, to garnish

handful of cherry tomatoes, halved, to serve

warmed pita or flatbreads, to serve

Prepare the falafel and ful moudamas (see pp. 98 and 194), ideally the day before. Cool and store, covered, in the fridge.

Preheat the oven to 300°F (150°C/130°C fan/gas 3). Warm the ful moudamas gently in a pan over low heat, then transfer to an ovenproof bowl and place in the oven. Wrap the falafel in foil and keep warm in the oven.

Heat 1 teaspoon of oil in a large frying pan and fry the halloumi for 1 to 2 minutes on each side until golden. Place on a plate and keep warm in the oven.

Heat the remaining oil in the same pan. Crack the eggs into the pan. Cook over gentle heat for 4 to 5 minutes until the whites are set, but the yolks are runny. To set the top, cover the pan with a lid for the last minute. Sprinkle with the sumac and sea salt.

Remove all the elements from the oven. Divide the eggs between 4 serving plates. Place a spoonful of labneh on each plate, sprinkle with za'atar, drizzle a little olive oil over, and top with an olive. Scatter a little parsley and oil over the ful moudamas and serve in the center of the table along with the falafel, halloumi, cherry tomatoes, and warmed bread for everybody to help themselves.

LEBANESE *tortilla*
with SAUSAGES

Lebanese sausages are cured beef sausages that are heavily spiced, generally with cumin and sumac; they can also be fairly hot. Although you can eat them as they are, as you would chorizo, they are quite hard and are best lightly cooked so that the fat releases its delicious flavors and the sausages soften. If you can't get hold of Lebanese ones, choose any spicy cured beef sausage, seasoned with chile, instead.

If you like a bit of richness and luxury at breakfast, then add the heavy cream to the egg mixture, and for an even heartier dish you could add a cold chopped potato to the pan before adding the eggs.

SERVES 1

2 small Lebanese sausages, chopped

1 tomato, quartered

2 large eggs

salt and freshly ground black pepper, to taste

2 tbsp chopped flat-leaf parsley

½ tsp ground cumin

⅓ cup (100ml) heavy cream (optional)

Heat a small frying pan, about 6 inches (15cm) in diameter, and fry the chopped sausages until golden and heated through. Add the tomato quarters to the pan and cook on each side.

Preheat the broiler to medium–high. Beat the eggs in a bowl and season well with salt and pepper. Stir in the parsley, cumin, and cream, if using. Pour the egg mixture into the pan and cook over medium heat until golden underneath.

Transfer the pan to the broiler and cook until puffed up and golden. Serve immediately.

Broad Bean DIP

Ful moudamas

Though it may seem strange, this spiced broad bean dip is served at breakfast time. With some warm pita or flatbreads, it makes a wholesome, nourishing start to the day, and the warmth from the spices gives you the pick-me-up that's often needed in the morning.

SERVES 4

1 (14-ounce/400g) can broad beans

1 tsp cumin seeds, toasted and lightly crushed

1 red chile, finely chopped (optional)

1 large ripe tomato, finely chopped

good drizzle of extra-virgin olive oil, plus extra to serve

salt

2 tbsp chopped flat-leaf parsley

warmed pita bread, to serve

Drain most of the liquid from the beans, leaving about 2 tablespoons behind. Put the beans and the liquid in a pan and add the cumin seeds, chile, if using, and tomato. Heat gently over medium heat for 3 to 4 minutes.

Pour into a large bowl, add a good drizzle of extra-virgin olive oil and season well with salt, then mash the beans until they have a creamy consistency.

Stir in the parsley, give it all a good pounding again, then serve with another good drizzle of oil and the warmed pita.

ch 8. *Breads*

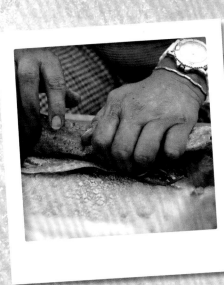

Breads

No self-respecting Lebanese cook would even consider serving their meal without some type of bread. Bread is essentially the backbone of our cuisine. So, whether it be pita bread as a vehicle for scooping up copious amounts of dips or sauces; saj bread for soaking up the juices of a pile of shawarma or koftas; warm cheese-and-lamb-topped man'ousha, or simply bread served warm from the oven, spread with a simple topping of za'atar mixed with olive oil for breakfast, bread will be on the table at every time of the day.

The problem is that while the word "flatbread," which is what most Middle Eastern breads are, makes it sound as though they would be simple to make, the fact is a huge amount of time and skill goes into producing the perfect bread we enjoy. Lebanese bread-making is all about the tossing, turning, and stretching of the dough — techniques that are developed with years of practice and experience and not skills you'll have perfected at home. So, with that in mind, the recipes in this chapter have been adapted so that you can re-create the essence of traditional Lebanese breads at home. Dan has even come up with a way of imitating an essential piece of a Lebanese baker's kit — the saj, a domed griddle over which the paper-thin stretched bread is baked. ●

PITA bread

Khobz araby

Pita is the essential bread to have on the table with all the food in this book, and it's something that I insist upon at Comptoir. Though pita isn't something you'd normally make yourself at home, it's worth trying if you've got an oven that can get fiery hot, as you'll need that to get the pita to puff up. This recipe is also a good, all-purpose flatbread dough and can be used for some of the flatbreads in this chapter. You can easily halve the quantity of dough if you don't want to make 10 breads.

MAKES ABOUT 10 PITA BREADS

1 1/3 to 1 2/3 cups (325 to 400ml) warm water

1 tsp instant yeast

2 tbsp olive oil

4 1/2 cups (600g) bread flour, plus extra for rolling the dough

1 tbsp superfine sugar

1 tsp salt

Pour the water into a mixing bowl, stir in the yeast until dissolved, then add the oil, flour, sugar, and salt. Mix everything to a fairly firm dough, adding extra water if the dough is a little dry, or extra flour if it's a little soft, then cover the bowl and set aside for 10 minutes. Lightly knead the dough until smooth, then return it to the bowl, cover, and set aside for 30 to 60 minutes, until slightly risen.

Heat the oven to 450°F (240°C/220°C fan/gas 9) and put a metal baking sheet inside. Divide the dough into 10 equal pieces, just under 3½ ounces (100g) each, and shape them into balls. Cover the balls, set aside for 15 minutes so they're easier to roll, then dust your work surface well with flour and roll half the balls out to rounds or ovals about 1/4 inch (5mm) thick. Make sure they're not sticking to the work surface, then cover with a clean dish towel and set aside for 10 minutes. Some bakers like to leave the rolled dough to sit on a well-floured wooden tray or a floured cloth, as the dough is less likely to stick to this.

Remove the baking sheet from the oven, place a few of the pita breads on it, then return to the oven and bake the pita for 4 to 5 minutes, until puffed and lightly colored. Remove from the baking sheet and cool on a wire rack or in a basket, covered with a clean cloth to keep them soft, then roll and bake the remaining dough.

PITA **bread**

TAHINI *butter* BUNS

There are days when I really crave a hamburger but want it with a kofta, or wonder what a hot dog bun would be like with a sausage-shaped kofta inside. So I asked Dan to make me a roll that would suit a kofta, and this is what he created. It's a little like a French "pain de mie" bread but with eggs and tahini, and it's excellent filled with salad, dips, and kebabs. These buns freeze brilliantly once baked, and you just thaw them and reheat briefly in the oven to return that just-baked softness.

MAKES ABOUT 10 BUNS

1 ²/₃ cups (400ml) milk

scant ¼ cup (50g) tahini (store-bought, or homemade, see p. 230), mixed well before measuring

1 egg, plus 1 beaten egg for brushing

3 egg yolks

1 (7g) package instant yeast

5 ¼ cups (700g) bread flour, plus extra for rolling the dough

1½ tbsp (25g) cornstarch

1½ tbsp (25g) superfine sugar

7 tbsp (100g) unsalted butter, cut into cubes

2 tsp salt

sesame or black onion (nigella) seeds, to finish

Bring the milk to a boil in a saucepan, then pour it into a large mixing bowl, whisk in the tahini, and set aside until warm. Beat in 1 whole egg, the 3 egg yolks, and the yeast, then add the flour, cornstarch, and sugar and mix to a fairly firm dough, adding a little water if the dough seems too dry or extra flour if it's too soft. You're aiming for a pliable dough that stretches and doesn't feel too soft and sticky.

Leave the dough in the bowl, covered, for 15 to 20 minutes, then place it on your work surface and roughly tear it open so you can work the butter through. Spread the butter cubes out over the dough, sprinkle with the salt, then aggressively work both together with your hands for about 5 minutes until the dough is smooth once more and no trace of butter can be seen. Then shape it back into a ball, return it to the bowl, cover, and set aside for about 90 minutes or until it has risen by half.

Divide the dough into 4½-ounce (125g) pieces and, using your hands, form into balls or long sausage shapes. Place them, spaced out, on baking sheets lined with parchment paper, cover, and set aside to rise until almost doubled.

Heat the oven to 400°F (200°C/180°C fan/gas 6). Brush the buns with the beaten egg and sprinkle with the sesame or black onion seeds, then bake the buns for about 25 minutes until golden on top.

SAJ BREAD

Khobz saj

My friend Kamal Mouzawak organizes a farmers' market in Beirut called the Souk el Tayeb, where families and farmers from the rural areas in Lebanon gather to sell their produce. It was here I met an extraordinary woman who was making sourdough flatbreads to sell. They were baked over a dome of metal, called a saj, and made with breathtaking speed from a simple dough of barley, white flour, and cornmeal, using a sourdough starter to slightly leaven and acidify the crumb. I've suggested using the same starter but if you don't have one you can mix together 1/2 cup (75g) whole wheat flour, ¼ cup plus 1 tablespoon (75ml) warm water, and a pinch of yeast and leave it covered for 2 days at room temperature: it won't have the same flavor but does the trick if you're in a rush.

I couldn't begin to explain how to shape the breads by hand in the air, as it's something I can't do, but you can make something similar with this recipe, created by Dan, which we use at Comptoir.

MAKES 8 TO 10 FLATBREADS

⅔ cup (200ml) warm water

5 ounces (150g) sourdough starter (or see above for how to make a substitute)

2 ¼ cups (275g) bread flour, plus extra for rolling the dough

1 ½ cups (200g) barley flour

1 ½ tbsp (25g) fine cornmeal

1 to 2 tsp salt

Pour the warm water into a large mixing bowl and dissolve the sourdough starter in it, breaking up any lumps with your fingers.

Add the bread flour, barley flour, cornmeal, and salt and mix well to a soft dough. Add more water if the dough seems dry, or extra flour if it's a bit wet. Cover the bowl and leave the dough for 1 to 2 hours, or until it starts to puff. At this point it's ready to use, or you can store it in the fridge for 1 to 2 days and use as needed.

To make the flatbreads, take a piece of dough the size of a small apple, and roll the dough out to about ⅛ inch (3mm) thick using extra flour to stop it from sticking to the work surface or the rolling pin. Have ready a large upturned wok placed over a ring on a gas stovetop.

When the wok is hot, lift the flatbread onto a large dinner plate and allow it to drape over the wok, watching that you don't burn yourself on the wok. When the dough starts to puff and scorch underneath, flip it over and cook the other side. Take the flatbread off with tongs, fold it into quarters, place it in a basket, and cover with a cloth, then repeat with the remaining dough. The cooked saj breads freeze very well in a sealable freezer bag. They are best defrosted by being wrapped in foil and then baked in an oven set at 400°F (200°C/180°C fan/gas 6), until hot throughout: this way they don't lose moisture and stay soft.

BLACK SEED &
halloumi FLATBREADS
Man'ousha jabneh

Man'ousha are best described as the Lebanese version of a small pizza. They are essentially flatbreads topped with za'atar, melted cheese, or meats and are most commonly served at breakfast. In Lebanon you'll find them in bakeries or made at home, where the simple dough recipe is prepared and then spread with the chosen topping before being baked.

For this recipe and the two other man'ousha recipes that follow we've suggested using our basic pita bread dough, and have given you some traditional toppings.

MAKES 6 FLATBREADS

½ recipe Pita Bread dough (see p. 202)

all-purpose flour, for rolling the dough

5 ounces (150g) halloumi, very thinly sliced

1 tsp sesame seeds

1 tsp black sesame seeds

salt

pinch of ground coriander

olive oil, for drizzling

leaves from a few sprigs of mint, to garnish

Preheat the oven to 425°F (220°C/200°C fan/gas 7). Put 2 large baking sheets in the oven to preheat.

Divide the pita dough into 6 equal pieces. Roll out each piece on a lightly floured board until it's about 6 inches (15cm) in diameter. Lay the pieces of halloumi on top and scatter the sesame seeds over them. Season with salt and the ground coriander then drizzle with a little oil.

Slide the man'ousha onto the baking sheets and bake in the oven for about 12 minutes, until the dough is crisp and the halloumi has melted.

Slide the man'ousha onto a board, scatter with the mint leaves, and serve while still warm.

Mini **LAMB** flatbreads

Laham bil ajeen

In Lebanon, you probably wouldn't find this slightly heavier man'ousha on the breakfast table, but it would be delicious served as part of a lunch spread with a light salad and a yogurt-based sauce or dip.

MAKES 6 FLATBREADS

1 small onion, grated

4 ounces (100g) ground lamb

2 tomatoes, finely chopped

generous pinch of dried chile flakes

½ tsp ground cinnamon

½ tsp ground allspice

1 tsp Lebanese 7-spice mix

1 tbsp pomegranate molasses

salt and freshly ground black pepper, to taste

½ recipe Pita Bread dough (see p. 200)

all-purpose flour, for rolling the dough

finely chopped flat-leaf parsley, to garnish

Preheat the oven to 425°F (220°C/200°C fan/gas 7). Put 2 baking sheets in the oven to preheat.

Put the onion, lamb, half the chopped tomatoes, the chile flakes, spices, molasses, and some salt and pepper into a food processor and process until finely chopped.

Divide the pita dough into 6 equal pieces. Roll out each piece on a lightly floured board until it's about 6 inches (15cm) in diameter.

Spoon the lamb mixture evenly over the 6 breads and use the back of a spoon to smooth it out over the dough. Slide the rounds onto the prepared baking sheets and bake in the oven for about 12 minutes, until the dough is golden and the topping is completely cooked.

Slide the flatbreads onto a board, scatter the remaining tomato over the bread, and garnish with the parsley. Serve warm.

ZA'ATAR *flatbreads*

Flatbreads are so simple and versatile. Here we've taken the basic pita dough recipe (p. 200) and used it to create an herby flatbread. In Lebanon, za'atar is the most common sight on the breakfast table, used as a light spread for toasted bread in the same way we use butter.

MAKES 6 FLATBREADS

for the sauce:

1 tbsp olive oil, plus extra for brushing

1 onion, finely chopped

2 to 3 tbsp za'atar, or to taste (store-bought, or homemade, see p. 186)

1 to 2 chopped tomatoes

salt and freshly ground black pepper, to taste

½ recipe Pita Bread dough (see p. 200)

all-purpose flour, for rolling the dough

olive oil, for brushing

small handful of chopped flat-leaf parsley

salt and freshly ground black pepper, to taste

¾ cup (150g) natural yogurt, to serve

mint leaves, chopped, to serve

Make the sauce first by heating the oil in a heavy-bottomed pan and sautéing the onion over low to medium heat for about 10 minutes, until it is softening and starting to turn golden.

Stir in the za'atar and cook for 1 to 2 minutes, then stir in the tomatoes and season well with salt. Cover with a lid and bring to a boil, then reduce the heat so the mixture is simmering and cook for 5 to 10 minutes. Taste to check the seasoning, then transfer to a food processor and process until smooth. Set aside.

Divide the pita dough into 6 rough pieces. Take 1 piece and divide it in half. Roll it out on a lightly floured board to make a thin round, about 4 inches (10cm) in diameter, then do the same with the other piece. Brush each piece with oil, then scatter some parsley over one half and season with salt and pepper. Place the other half on top and roll it again to flatten and fuse the 2 sides together. Do the same with the other pieces of dough to make 6 rounds in total.

Heat a griddle pan until hot. Lay a couple of rounds of dough on the griddle. Cook for a couple of minutes, pressing down slightly with a metal spatula until the dough has cooked and has turned golden. Flip over and continue to cook on the other side. Do the same with the remaining pieces of dough.

Pour the tomato sauce into a bowl, top with the yogurt and mint, and serve alongside the toasted flatbreads.

Ch 9. *Soups*, sauces **&** pickles

COMPTOIR LIBANAIS

Soups, sauces & pickles

This probably sounds like the least sexy chapter in the book, but soups, sauces, and pickles are such an important part of Lebanese cuisine that I'd urge you not to overlook it.

I love making soups. They're so easy to bring together, yet they are healthy, filling, and delicious. What's more, they are best combined with another one of my great food loves — bread — so they give me the perfect excuse to serve up warm flatbreads, toasted pita, or my favorite: pita chips — crunchy little squares of bread that can be flavored by frying them with a little garlic or za'atar. To make your own breads, or for more substantial bread-based accompaniments, turn to the Breads chapter on p. 196.

Sauces are another fundamental part of a meal and are used abundantly in Lebanon — whether chile- or spice-based to add a layer of flavor to a dish, or yogurt-based as a cooling counterfoil. The tahini sauce needs little introduction; it's like the Lebanese equivalent of mayonnaise or ketchup — a pantry staple.

Pickles are everywhere in Lebanon; they appear on every table. They are great as a snack, paired with dips, or as a really zingy addition to mezze. ●

LENTIL soup

Shorbat adas

This hearty soup is another dish that is prepared throughout the Middle East and that's often cooked during Ramadan as the lentils are nourishing, satisfying, and sustaining. This recipe is quite filling as it is, but if you like really thick soups you could increase the quantity of lentils to 1¼ cups (250g). If you're serving this as a main dish, the crispy pita "chips" are not only a wonderful way of adding texture, but also of filling it out more.

SERVES 6 AS A STARTER OR 4 AS A MAIN

1 tbsp olive oil, plus extra for frying the pita breads

1 onion, finely chopped

salt and freshly ground black pepper, to taste

1 garlic clove, crushed

1 tsp ground cumin

1 cup (200g) red lentils

1 quart (1 liter) hot vegetable or chicken stock

squeeze of lemon juice

2 pita breads

Heat the oil in a heavy-bottomed pan and add the onion. Season with salt and pepper and fry over low heat for about 15 minutes, until soft.

Stir in the garlic and cumin and cook for 1 minute. Stir in the red lentils, making sure they're thoroughly coated in the softened onions, and allow them to heat gently in the base of the pan.

Pour in the stock and bring to a boil. Reduce the heat and simmer for 15 minutes until the lentils are soft. Cool a little, then whiz in a food processor or blender until smooth. Return the soup to the pan and stir in the lemon juice. Check the seasoning and gently reheat.

Toast the pita breads, then break them into pieces. Heat a little oil in a pan and fry the toasted pita bread pieces in the oil, until they are crispy and some are beginning to turn a deep golden brown around the edges.

Ladle the soup into serving bowls and serve with the pita "chips."

Pumpkin SOUP

Shorbat lakten

The texture of this soup is so velvety, it feels like it has cream in it, but in fact it's a healthy mixture of vegetables, and the creaminess comes from the silky texture of the pumpkin. It's flavored with a collection of Lebanese spices, but if, like me, you like a kick of heat, add a whole dried chile to the stock while it is simmering. It's not traditional but I think it gives it a great punch.

SERVES 6 TO 8

2 tbsp olive oil, plus extra to serve

1 onion, finely chopped

1 garlic clove, crushed

1 celery stalk, finely chopped

1 small carrot, finely chopped

salt and freshly ground black pepper, to taste

2 pounds (900g) pumpkin or butternut squash, peeled, deseeded, and chopped

seeds from 3 cardamom pods, crushed

pinch of ground cinnamon

pinch of freshly grated nutmeg

5 cups (1.2 liters) hot vegetable or chicken stock

to serve:

tahini, for drizzling

olive oil, for drizzling

za'atar (store-bought, or homemade, see p. 186), for sprinkling

small handful of chopped flat-leaf parsley

toasted bread

Heat the oil in a heavy-bottomed pan and add the onion, garlic, celery, and carrot. Season well with salt and pepper and gently sauté over low heat for 10 to 15 minutes until softened and starting to turn golden.

Stir in the pumpkin or squash and the cardamom, cinnamon, and nutmeg and cook for a couple of minutes to warm the vegetables through and toast the spices.

Pour in the stock, cover with a lid, and bring to a boil. Simmer for around 15 minutes until the vegetables are soft. Leave to cool a little, then transfer to a blender and whiz until smooth. Return the soup to the pan, check the seasoning, and reheat gently.

To serve, divide between serving bowls. Drizzle with tahini and olive oil, then sprinkle za'atar and parsley over the top. Serve with the bread.

Garlic SAUCE

Toum

An utterly intense garlic sauce. Use it sparingly unless you love a big hit of garlic like I do. Serve it with any grilled meat dish.

MAKES ABOUT 1 CUP (200G)

15 large garlic cloves, crushed

½ tsp salt

¼ cup plus 1 tbsp (about 75ml) lemon juice

¼ cup plus 1 tbsp (about 75ml) olive oil

Place the garlic in a blender with the salt and half the lemon juice, and purée until quite smooth, stopping the blender often to scrape down the sides. Then add half the olive oil and purée again on high until the mixture forms a smooth, light cream. Slowly add more oil, a spoonful at a time, and purée until the mixture begins to thicken. Then add a little more lemon juice to thin it. Alternate between the two until you have a thick, utterly light cream. Store in the fridge.

TAHINI *sauce*

Tarator

This is the sauce you find anywhere and everywhere in Lebanon. It's an absolute must with the broiled dishes, particularly drizzled over a shawarma (see p. 132), but the Lebanese will basically find any excuse to serve it with their meals.

MAKES ABOUT ¾ CUP (150G)

¼ cup tahini

good pinch of salt

up to a scant ½ cup (100ml) cold water

squeeze of lemon juice

Put the tahini in a bowl and stir in the salt. Pour in half the cold water then work the water into the tahini. Gradually work in more water until the mixture has the consistency of very thick cream; you may not need to use all the water. Stir in the lemon juice and taste for seasoning before serving.

Homemade TAHINI paste

Tahina

If you don't have tahini but can get ahold of sesame seeds, this is an easy way to make your own paste. The resulting paste has a slightly stronger flavor, a darker color, and is slightly thinner than store-bought tahini. To turn it into a sauce to serve with grilled meats or falafel, or drizzled on soups or as a dressing for salads, see p. 228.

MAKES ABOUT 1 CUP (175G)

¾ cup (100g) sesame seeds, white or natural

¼ cup plus 1 tbsp (75ml) light olive or sunflower oil

Place the seeds in a heavy-bottomed pan with half the oil, and heat until the seeds sizzle. Cook for a few minutes until they lose their raw color and are just beginning to lightly brown, then spoon into a bowl and allow to cool slightly.

When cool, tip the seeds into a blender, add a little of the remaining oil, and purée on a high speed for a few minutes. At first it'll need lots of scraping down but as the seeds become crushed they'll release their oil and the purée will become thinner. Add slightly more of the reserved oil, purée again, and continue until the mixture is very smooth and creamy.

Pour the tahini into a jar with a tight-fitting lid, seal, then store in the fridge and use as required.

Yogurt, chile, and DRIED mint sauce

Much of European cuisine uses cream as the starting ingredient in its sauces to provide richness and viscosity, but I think the Middle Eastern alternative — yogurt — is a far superior base, particularly when you think of the flavor profile of our food. Not only is yogurt much healthier, but its sourness is a perfect contrast to the sweetness found in certain common Lebanese spices, such as cinnamon and allspice.

This yogurt-based sauce is so easy to throw together, and it's something that can be used in so many contexts: as a dressing for grilled lamb, chicken shawarma, or pan-fried fish, or even stirred through vegetables to create an interesting and refreshing salad. Add as much heat as you like, then soften it with the seasonings of lemon and mint. A good pinch of salt will seal the deal.

MAKES ABOUT ½ CUP (125G)

½ tsp dried mint

1 tsp cider vinegar

½ cup (100ml) full-fat natural yogurt

1 tbsp olive oil

squeeze of lemon juice

pinch of dried chile flakes

salt and freshly ground black pepper, to taste

Put the dried mint in a bowl and stir in the cider vinegar. Add the remaining ingredients and whisk together, seasoning to taste. Store in a sealed container in the fridge and use within 5 days.

CHILE paste

Here's a very hot paste that you will find yourself using in lots of different savory recipes. It's a must spread on a wrap with a chicken kofta, or it can just as easily be used stirred into yogurt and drizzled over crisp vegetables for a kick of heat in a salad.

MAKES ENOUGH FOR 12 SERVINGS

4 red bell peppers

15 red chiles

2 garlic cloves, crushed

2 tbsp olive oil

⅔ cup (200ml) water

Cut the bell peppers in half and remove the core, seeds, and any white pith from the inside. Roughly chop the flesh and put it in a food processor.

Trim the stalks from the chiles, then halve the chiles. Roughly chop the chiles, then add them to the food processor along with the garlic. Process all the ingredients together to chop them finely.

Heat the oil in a large, heavy-bottomed pan. Add the pepper mixture and sauté for about 10 minutes. Pour the water into the pan and continue to cook, stirring every now and then to ensure the chopped vegetables don't stick to the bottom. Cook until the mixture has thickened.

Put half of the chile paste into a sterilized jar (see p. 60), seal, then store in the fridge and use within 5 days. Put the remaining half into a freezer container, seal, and freeze for up to 3 months.

NATURAL pickle *brine*

Pickling is one of the oldest methods of food preservation. It can be done in two ways, either by placing vegetables in a brine solution, which produces lactic acid and conserves the vegetables, or by placing them directly in an acidic liquid, usually vinegar. Sometimes both are used together. This brine contains a little vinegar, enough to get the lactic bacteria started and to help the fermentation stay sour.

MAKES 1 QUART (1 LITER)

¼ cup (50g) sea salt (don't use table salt as it's too bitter)

⅔ cup (200ml) boiling water

3 ¼ cups (800ml) cold water

1 tsp cider vinegar

Dissolve the salt in the boiling water, then add the cold water and vinegar. Make sure you don't stick your fingers in the liquid at any point; use clean tongs or a spoon to keep bacteria out. I use a deep, oblong plastic container with a sealable lid as a brining container, washed clean just before using.

Pickled CUCUMBER

MAKES 1 LARGE JAR

2 pounds (about 850g) small cucumbers, peeled and cut into 2-inch (5cm) fingers

8 to 10 garlic cloves

1 to 2 tsp dried chile flakes

1 recipe Natural Pickle Brine (see above)

Place the cucumbers in a clean container, pour the brine over them, then cover the container and leave for 20 days.

PICKLED TURNIPS and BEETS

Kabees

Turnips are often pickled with beets, which gives them a lovely rosy tint. At first this may not seem like enough beets in comparison to the turnips, but after a few days, when the fermentation begins, the color will be drawn out, gradually getting darker over the 20 days until the liquid turns a deep purple color.

SERVES 6

1¼ pounds (550g) turnips
(about 4)

2 tbsp (25g) salt

1 raw beet, peeled

8 to 10 garlic cloves

2 tsp superfine sugar

1 recipe Natural Pickle Brine
(see p. 236)

Slice the tops and tails off the turnips and peel them if you like. Cut them into quarters or slices. Typically we don't mix the cuts up, just choose one you prefer. Place the turnips in a bowl, mix with the salt, and leave overnight.

The next day, discard the liquid released from the turnips, and rinse the turnips under running water to remove the excess salt.

Cut the beet into slices to help the color bleed, then place in a brining container along with the garlic and turnips. Dissolve the sugar in the natural pickle brine, pour it over the turnips, seal the container, and leave for 20 days at room temperature, then store in the fridge for 4 to 6 weeks.

ch 10. *Sweets,* desserts **&** jams

Sweets, desserts & jams

Middle Easterners are famous for their love of very sweet things, and pastry shops are a common sight across the Levant, their windows glistening with the shiny glaze of the sweet treats, drawing you in. Although this type of sweetmeat could be served at the end of the meal, you are more likely to find them being served mid-morning or afternoon, accompanied by a bitter Arabic coffee or a refreshing mint tea.

Desserts, too, are rich with sweetness, often sticky with honey and syrups made from fruit or rosewater, or thick and creamy when based around yogurt, rice, or sweetened cheeses. Texture is an important component in these desserts, so you will find the silky smoothness of a cheesecake or ice cream contrasted with a scattering of *crunchy pistachios over the top. This chapter will give you the chance to experiment with a range of desserts and sweet treats, some very traditional and others, such as the Plum Cheesecake (see p. 252), which simply use Lebanese ingredients within the context of a dessert that's perhaps more Western in origin.* ●

ROSE MARZIPAN-*stuffed* DATES *with yogurt*

Lebanese sweets are rich but they are nevertheless served piled high and plentiful. Enjoy them with dark Arabica coffee or mint tea at the end of a meal or mid-morning or afternoon snack.

If you want to use ready-made marzipan in this recipe you'll need 7 ounces (200g); just knead in a little rosewater to flavor it before coloring. Similarly, if the perfumed flavor of rose isn't your thing, you can leave it out and just make plain marzipan — the dates will be just as sweet and tasty.

MAKES 12

12 Medjool dates

¼ cup plus 1 tbsp (50g) confectioners' sugar, plus extra for kneading

2 tbsp (25g) superfine sugar, plus 2 to 3 tbsp for dusting

1 cup (100g) ground almonds

1 tsp lemon juice

1 tsp rosewater

a little green food coloring

a little red food coloring

natural yogurt, to serve

Slice down the length of each date and carefully pry them apart. Remove the pits, then open each date wide enough to fill with the marzipan. Set aside.

To make the marzipan, sift the confectioners' sugar into a bowl, then stir in the superfine sugar and ground almonds. Make a well in the center of the mixture and pour in the lemon juice and rosewater. Mix everything together until the mixture looks crumbly. Then bring it together with your hands to make a dough.

Divide the dough into 3 equal pieces. Take 1 piece and divide it into 4, then shape each piece into an oval. Fill each date with a piece of marzipan. Make a pattern by marking lines along the marzipan with a knife.

Fill a small saucer with superfine sugar and press the marzipan into it. Set these dates aside to dry while you fill the remaining ones.

Take another piece of marzipan and knead in a few dots of green food coloring until you achieve the desired color. Divide it into 4, as before, then fill the dates. Mark and push into the sugar to coat.

Use the same method with the last piece of marzipan, coloring it red and filling the dates in exactly the same way.

The dates will soon dry. When dry, store them in an airtight container in a cool place for up to 5 days. Serve with yogurt.

COMPTOIR FROZEN yogurt

The rich, silky texture of this frozen yogurt is achieved by churning in an ice-cream machine. If you don't have one, it's still relatively easy to make. Put the tub in the freezer, then whisk every hour or so until firm.

SERVES 4

2½ cups (500g) full-fat yogurt (Greek yogurt works well)

¼ cup (50g) superfine sugar

1 tsp vanilla extract

to serve:

(top) 1 tbsp clear honey and 1 tbsp chopped, roasted mixed nuts

or

(bottom left) a small piece of crumbled halva and a few roasted pistachios

or

(bottom right) a handful of pomegranate seeds, a few sprigs of mint, and a drop or two of orange blossom water

Stir all the ingredients together in a bowl, then transfer to an ice-cream machine and churn according to the manufacturer's instructions until thick, icy, and almost frozen. Scrape into a freezer container and freeze until firm. Serve with the topping of your choice.

PUMPKIN, SESAME, AND LABNEH *tart*

This beautiful sweet custard tart showcases some of the best Levantine produce. The pastry dough is made with tahini, which gives it a gentle and subtle sesame seed flavor, and the tart filling contains labneh and pomegranate molasses. It is equally good served warm or cold with ice cream and honey.

Baking a pumpkin is easy, as you cut it into manageable chunks, then wrap them all in foil and bake for 20 to 35 minutes until tender. The recipe makes double the amount of pastry, but you can freeze it. And if you have any leftover filling you could put it in ramekins and bake it separately — it makes a lovely dessert on its own, served with ice cream.

MAKES 1 (8-INCH/20CM) TART, SERVES 6 TO 8

for the pastry:

2 cups (250g) all-purpose flour, plus extra for rolling out

¼ cup plus 1 tbsp (50g) confectioners' sugar

¾ cup (150g) unsalted butter, cut into cubes

1 ½ tbsp (25g) tahini

3 tbsp plain yogurt

2 egg yolks

3 tbsp (25g) toasted sesame seeds (see p. 252)

for the filling:

½ pound (200g) pumpkin flesh, baked and drained of any liquid (see above)

½ cup (100g) labneh (see p. 58)

¼ cup (100g) clear honey

¼ cup (75g) pomegranate molasses

5 egg yolks

sesame seeds, to finish

Preheat the oven to 325°F (170°C/150°C fan/gas 3). Grease an 8-inch (20cm) tart tin.

For the pastry, measure the flour, sugar, and butter into a bowl and rub it with your fingers (or use a food processor) until the butter disappears and the mixture is crumbly. Add the tahini, yogurt, egg yolks, and sesame seeds, mix everything together into a very soft paste, then pat it into a rectangular shape on a sheet of parchment paper or plastic wrap. Wrap well and chill for about 30 minutes, until firm. Return to room temperature just before using.

On a lightly floured board or work surface, roll the pastry out to about ⅛ inch (3mm) thick and carefully line the base and sides of the tart tin with the dough. Chill for 20 minutes, then line the bottom with parchment paper, cover with pie weights or dried beans, and blind bake for 30 to 35 minutes, removing the paper and weights for the last 5 to 10 minutes of baking so that the pastry shell dries out and turns golden.

For the filling, mash the pumpkin, labneh, honey, molasses, and egg yolks until smooth (or use a food processor). Spoon just enough into the tart shell to almost fill it — then sprinkle with sesame seeds and bake for about 25 minutes until just gently puffed. Set aside to cool a little before serving the tart warm.

Plum *cheesecake*

This recipe combines a European favouite with some of the best flavors of Lebanese desserts – stone fruit, oranges and pistachio nuts. Note that this cheesecake needs to be chilled overnight, so you should make it the day before you want to serve it.

SERVES 16

for the base:

4 tbsp (50g) butter, melted, plus extra for greasing the pan

4 ½ ounces (125g) Carr's Whole Wheat Crackers or digestive biscuits

for the filling:

32 ounces (900g) full-fat cream cheese

½ cup plus 2 tbsp (150ml) heavy cream

¾ cup plus 2 tbsp (175g) superfine sugar

3 eggs

juice of 1 lemon

for the topping:

8 plums, quartered

¾ cup (150g) sugar

juice of 1 orange

1 tbsp (15g) pistachio nuts, chopped

To make the base, preheat the oven to 300°F (150°C/130°C fan/gas 2). Grease a deep 8-inch (20cm) square cake pan with butter and line it with parchment paper.

Put the crackers in a food processor and pulse briefly to break down the pieces. Alternatively you could crush them by hand by putting them in a freezer bag and bashing them with a rolling pin. Pour the crushed crackers into a bowl and add the melted butter. Stir well to mix the ingredients together, then spoon into the prepared cake pan. Level the surface with the back of a spoon, and bake in the oven for 10 minutes. Remove and set aside to cool; leave the oven on.

To make the filling, spoon the cream cheese into a bowl. Pour in the heavy cream and sugar, then beat everything together. In a separate, clean bowl, beat the eggs and stir in half the lemon juice. Gradually beat this mixture into the cream cheese mixture, alternating with a drizzle of the remaining lemon juice each time. Beat until smooth.

Spoon the filling over the base in the cake pan and bake in the oven for 1 hour, turning the pan every now and then so the mixture colors evenly on all sides. Turn the oven off and leave the cheesecake to cool in the oven for 1 hour.

Remove from the oven and set aside to cool completely, then transfer to the fridge and chill overnight.

To make the topping, put the plums, sugar, and orange juice in a pan, cover with a lid, and bring to a gentle boil. Turn down the heat and simmer for 5 to 8 minutes until the fruit has softened. Remove from the heat and set aside to cool a little.

Lift the cheesecake out of the pan and cut it into even squares. Spoon a couple of pieces of plum and some syrup over each piece, scatter with the pistachios, and serve.

Lebanese *date* PASTRIES

Maamoul

These cookies, known as maamoul, are one of my favorite sweets at Comptoir. They have a slightly coarse and delicately sweet semolina butter pastry that surrounds a filling of dates or walnuts, and are simply dusted with confectioners' sugar. The traditional recipe calls for the dough to sit overnight, and we think it gives the best result.

MAKES ABOUT 18 INDIVIDUAL PASTRIES, OR 1 (7-INCH/18CM) SQUARE TIN

for the dough:

¾ cup (150g) unsalted butter

2 cups (300g) fine semolina

¼ tsp salt

¼ cup plus 2 tbsp (75g) superfine sugar

2 to 3 drops almond extract, or ¼ tsp ground mahlab

1½ tbsp (25ml) orange blossom water

1½ tbsp (25ml) rosewater

1 tsp instant yeast

for the date filling:

10½ ounces (300g) pitted dried dates

4 tbsp (50g) unsalted butter, softened

½ tsp ground cinnamon

shelled peeled pistachios, chopped or sliced (optional)

confectioners' sugar, to finish

The night before you want to make the pastries, heat the butter in a heavy-bottomed saucepan until most of the milky solids have disappeared from the bottom, then remove from the heat. Put the semolina in a bowl then stir in the melted butter, mixing well. Cover the bowl and leave overnight at room temperature.

The following day, mix in the salt, sugar, almond extract or mahlab, orange water, and rosewater. Dissolve the yeast in 1 tablespoon of warm water, then add it to the bowl. Cover the bowl and set aside for 1 to 2 hours at room temperature before using.

For the filling, purée the dates, butter, and cinnamon until smooth.

TO MAKE INDIVIDUAL DATE PASTRIES
Preheat the oven to 325°F (160°C/140°C fan/gas 2½).

For each pastry, take 2 tablespoons (30g) of dough and roll it into a ball. Place the ball in the palm of one hand, then press into the ball to make a hollow almost through to the other side. Place 1 tablespoon (20g) of date filling inside, push the pastry gently up around it with your thumb, then pinch the seams gently to seal it. Place on a baking sheet lined with parchment paper, seam-end down, and press the tines of a fork 4 or 5 times around the sides to make grooves.

Bake the pastries for 25 to 30 minutes, or until just beginning to brown on the base and very top. Set aside to cool completely, then dust well with confectioners' sugar, and serve.

If you would like to add a crunchy coating of pistachio to your pastries, just press chopped or slivered pistachios onto the outside of the dough and bake in the same way. If you want very green pistachios, blanch the shelled nuts in boiling water for 15 minutes, then peel the skins off, as this both reveals and intensifies the green color.

Date JAM

This rich and sticky jam is seriously addictive when spread on hot toast, but it could be used in so many different ways. Serve it as an accompaniment to natural yogurt or labneh (see p. 56) or with pancakes for breakfast, or you could even try using it as you would a chutney, with cheese or hummus.

MAKES ABOUT 2 CUPS (500G)

about 1 pound (400g) dried dates, roughly chopped

1 ²/₃ cups (400ml) water

½ tsp ground cloves

½ tsp ground ginger

½ tsp ground cinnamon

juice of 1 lemon

2 tbsp (25g) granulated sugar

finely grated zest of 1 orange

1 cup (100g) toasted and roughly chopped almonds (optional)

1 tsp aniseeds (optional)

Put the dates into a pan with the water. Bring to a boil and simmer for around 5 minutes, until softened. Stir in the spices, lemon juice, and sugar.

Gently return to a boil. Reduce the heat to low, then simmer for 8 to 10 minutes, until the mixture is thick. Add the orange zest and, if you like, the almonds and aniseeds, then simmer for a few more minutes.

Spoon hot into sterilized jars (see note on p. 60) and seal with lids. Store in a cool, dark place and refrigerate after opening.

FIG jam

The concept of separating sweet and savory does not really exist in Middle Eastern cooking as it does in typical British cuisine. The food there loves to combine the two — hence, you'll find a sweet, syrupy pomegranate molasses used in dishes you might think of as inherently savory, such as the fried chicken livers on p. 114. Figs are one ingredient that are used as often in a savory context as in a sweet, so this rich, dense jam could just as easily be served as an accompaniment to a savory mezze selection — it's particularly good with labneh — as it would be scooped up with a flatbread for breakfast.

If you're lucky enough to have a fig tree near you, pick the figs that are still green and just yield to the touch for this jam — they will just be about to ripen and so will have the best and strongest flavor.

MAKES ABOUT 1½ CUPS (350G)

about ½ pound (200g) green figs
juice of 1 lemon
1 cup (200g) granulated sugar

Cut off and discard the tops of the figs, then roughly chop the fruit. Put them in a medium pan and add the lemon juice. Bring to a simmer and cook gently for 5 minutes to soften the fruit.

Add the sugar and heat gently until it dissolves. As soon as the sugar has dissolved, bring the mixture to a boil, and simmer over low to medium heat for around 5 minutes, until the mixture is jammy. There should still be a little liquid in the mixture – this will thicken as it cools.

Transfer to a sterilized jar (see p. 60), and seal. Store in a cool, dark place. Once opened, store in the fridge and enjoy within a month.

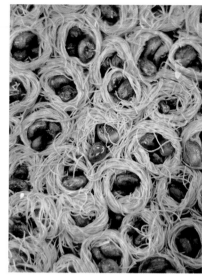

ch 11. *Drinks*

Pomegranate & *orange blossom* lemonade

The color of this juice is reason enough to make up a jug, as it's incredibly striking. The juice is easy to make and as the fruit is naturally sweet the recipe calls for very little sugar – simply add enough for your own taste.

SERVES 4

8 large pomegranates

4 to 6 tsp superfine sugar, or more to taste

juice of 2 to 3 lemons

2 tsp orange blossom water

Cut each pomegranate in half. Tap the hard side of the skin firmly with a wooden spoon, which should release the seeds. Remove any that remain in the shell and discard any white pith that's stuck to the seeds.

Set a generous handful of seeds to one side, then put the remainder into a food processor with the sugar, lemon juice, and orange blossom water and pulse together. Strain through a sieve, then pour into a jug.

Add a few spoonfuls of crushed ice.

Top with the reserved pomegranate seeds and serve.

FRESH LEMON
& *lime lemonade*

The Lebanese coastline is scattered with citrus orchards, the produce of which is one of Lebanon's main exports, so it follows that lemonade is commonly served as a refreshing, cooling drink. This recipe makes a tart citrus cordial that is simply topped up with water when you need it. It will keep in the fridge for up to one month.

SERVES 4

scant ½ cup (100ml) freshly squeezed lemon juice

scant ¼ cup (50ml) freshly squeezed lime juice

finely grated zest of 2 lemons, ideally unwaxed

½ cup plus 2 tbsp (about 125g) superfine sugar

to serve:

crushed ice

chopped mint leaves

cold water

The night before serving, place the juices, zest, and sugar in a jug and stir well, then cover and leave overnight in the refrigerator. This lemon juice syrup will preserve the fresh flavor of the juice. It will keep, chilled, for 1–2 weeks.

To serve, place 3 to 4 tablespoons of the lemon juice syrup per person in a jug, add crushed ice and mint, then stir well. Add just enough water to keep the flavor tart, then serve.

Rose LEMONADE

Different but delicious, this fragrant drink makes an interesting alternative to a classic lemonade. And when the British roses come out, it's the perfect refresher to enjoy on a hot summer's day.

MAKES ¾ CUP (200ML)

1 cup (200g) granulated sugar

juice of 2 lemons

large handful of unsprayed red rose petals (optional)

2 to 3 tbsp rosewater or rose syrup

chilled water, for serving

Put the sugar in a pan. Add the lemon juice and heat gently to dissolve the sugar.

Add the rose petals and bring to a boil. Simmer for 3 to 4 minutes, then stir in the rosewater.

Strain through a sieve and pour into a sterilized bottle, then chill.

To serve, pour a tablespoon of the rose-lemon syrup into a glass and top with chilled water.

Lebanese wine & arak
by Michael Karam

Michael Karam is an authority on Lebanese wines and spirits, and author of **The Wines of Lebanon** *and* **Arak and Mezze: The Taste of Lebanon**, *both of which discuss the relationship between food and drink in the Lebanese kitchen.*

I DOUBT VERY MANY PEOPLE KNOW THAT LEBANON IS ONE OF THE world's oldest sites of wine production and a country with an intimate relationship with the vine. However, despite its 7,000-year wine heritage, the modern industry really began in the mid-nineteenth century and continued during the country's period of French administration during the first half of the twentieth century.

Today Lebanon's most popular grape varieties – Cabernet Sauvignon, Merlot, Mourvèdre, Grenache, Syrah, Chardonnay, Sauvignon Blanc, Viognier, Muscat, Semillon, Riesling, Ugni Blanc, and Clairette – reflect this Francophone heritage.

There are indigenous grape varieties, however, and when wine experts come to Lebanon they're usually on the lookout for the white Obaideh and Merwah, simply because they are authentic Lebanese grapes and give a unique identity to the wines they produce. They can be found in the iconic and quirky Château Musar whites as well as those produced by Domaine Wardy and Massaya. Lebanon does not have its own red grape, but the Cinsault grape has been in Lebanon for more than 150 years, so we have unofficially adopted it as our own.

But arguably the drink that most typifies the Lebanese is arak, our national drink. An anise-flavored, triple-distilled spirit, traditionally made from Obaideh, it's similar to Greek ouzo or Turkish raki. It is also made from what many believe is the finest aniseed in the world, grown in the foothills of Mount Hermon, in Syria, in a village called Hina.

During the arak-making season, there is a great sense of fellowship within Lebanon's rural communities. People pick the grapes together, crush the grapes together, then finally sit around together while the grape juice distills. The fact that arak is drunk with mezze is a very natural and quite lovely evolution of a journey that begins on the vine and ends up on the Lebanese table.

Arak has palate-cleansing qualities that allow you to move from dish to dish with a "fresh mouth." In this way, it is the perfect accompaniment to Lebanese food. How much arak one puts in the glass depends on personal taste. Some people mix it half-and-half with water but I prefer one third arak to two thirds water: "tilt bi tiltain," as we say in Arabic. If you wish, you can flavor it by dropping a few fresh mint leaves on top.

There's also a sense of ritual to drinking arak. It should be drunk from a small tumbler or kes, which should be changed after each round. There is also an order to the preparation: arak, water, then the ice.

Do try arak if you want the sense of the authentic with your Lebanese dining, but if you prefer the idea of wine, keep it light and fruity. Then again, there is no reason why you can't simply have juice or water. It is this respect for the individual that typifies the Lebanese meal, which is pressure-free and convivial, like the menu, from which there is so much to choose. Sahtein! MK

Lebanese COFFEE

The coffee served in Lebanon is very similar to Turkish coffee — thick and very strong. While the Turks may add rose- or orange water to it, in Lebanon coffee is often flavored with cardamom. It is typically served in small, espresso-size portions, and once you've tried it you will understand why. If you're not used to it, it can be a pretty strong hit.

Coffee is served throughout the day, and when somebody drops in for a visit, unquestionably it will be coffee that's offered to them. The strong, slightly bitter flavor makes a perfect contrast to Lebanese sweet pastries, and meals will always end with the brewing of a pot of coffee. Sugar is added to the coffee while it is being brewed, so if you're preparing it traditionally you will need to find out if your guests would like it sweetened before preparing the coffee. And for true authenticity, try and source the traditional long-handled pot — a rakwe.

SERVES 3 TO 4

3 to 4 tsp Lebanese coffee

sugar, to taste

ground cardamom, to taste (optional)

Use ¼ cup (60ml) of water per teaspoon of coffee. Place the water and coffee in a rakwe or pan, then bring to a boil. Lower the heat to a simmer then turn off the heat and leave the coffee to settle for 3 to 5 minutes before serving. If sugar is required, add it to the pot as the water is coming to a boil. For a beautiful aroma and flavor, go whole hog and add a pinch of cardamom to the pot, too.

Mint TEA

Mint tea is another staple across North Africa and the Middle East, where it is served as a refreshing, reviving drink throughout the day with meals or simply as a moment's break. The recipe I've given here is for a traditional method, made with green tea as well as mint – fresh or dried. It's traditionally served very sweet, but I'll leave that up to you.

SERVES 2

2 tsp loose green tea leaves or 1 green teabag

6 fresh mint leaves, or 2 tsp dried mint leaves

sugar, to taste

a few drops of rosewater (optional)

Steep the tea and mint in 2 cups of freshly boiled water for several minutes, then add sugar to taste. In Lebanon, tea is served very sweet, so a lot of sugar is added, but I prefer to add a few drops of rosewater.

WASSIM AL SAMMOUR *was born in Damascus, Syria, and trained at the **Meridian**, **Sheraton**, and **Omayad** hotels. In Dubai, Wassim was the Lebanese chef at the **Jebel Ali Hotel**. Wassim moved to London in 1999 for work at the **Hilton Park Lane** and was chef for the Lebanese buffet. Today he is the head chef at **Levant**, and in charge of special events for **Comptoir Libanais**.*

DAVID JONES *has worked as a chef in Morocco, the Caribbean, and Istanbul, as well as opening 6 restaurants in the UK. Born in Sheffield, David started his training in restaurants and hotels in Yorkshire, then began a stellar career spanning 5-star restaurants as well as modern "pop-up" eateries. He is the former head chef of **Levant** and now the executive chef for **Comptoir Libanais** and the **Levant Group**. Whether at home cooking with his Persian wife, Katounya, or at Comptoir, David is fanatical about Lebanese and Middle Eastern food.*

DAN LEPARD *is an award-winning chef, author, and food photographer, whose first book,* **Baking with Passion**, *was published in 1999. He photographed Giorgio Locatelli's masterwork* **Made In Italy**, *winner of the Glenfiddich and World Gourmand awards, and* **Hawksmoor At Home**, *as well as his own books,* **The Handmade Loaf** *and* **Short & Sweet** *(winner of the Andre Simon Award). Born in Melbourne, Dan now spends most of his time in London, cooking, writing about, and photographing food.*

RANA SALAM *is one of the most celebrated graphic designers and artists from the Middle East. Rana has been running her own London- and now Beirut-based design studio for more than a decade, producing distinctive designs for her clients. Her unique knowledge of Arab culture and its popular art stems from years of travelling and documenting. Rana worked closely with Comptoir Libanais and Tony Kitous on the design of every element of the restaurant's look and feel, capturing the authentic atmosphere of the Middle East. Rana art-directed and styled this cookbook, working closely with Neal Townsend.*

acknowledgments

I would like to thank so many people who have helped me in my life and in making this book happen. Here are a few of them: Chaker Hanna, Trevor Dolby, Katherine Murphy, Phil Brown, Neal Townsend, Dan Lepard, David Whitehouse, Rana Salam, Imogen Fortes, Emma Marsden, Nicola Ibison, Q.R., Jean-Pierre Lentini, Babette Colin, Alexander Corrigan (RIP), Mamdouh Ismail, Amr Ismail, Moteia Ismail, Ali Aneizi, Daphne Lerner, Mohab Mufti, Haleem Kherallah, Ziad El-Akabi, Stella Goldman, Kamal Mouzawak, Michael Karam, Karim Haidar, Christine Mason, Jan Glen, David Jones, Wassim Al-Sammour, Asmaa Hassouni, Othman Bahnini, Saleh Al Geziry, Anwer Piracha, Danny Dawson, Sue Crozier, Tracey Mills, Trevor Shelley (RIP), Simon Binder, Nickolas Kalamaras, Aku Patel, Garth Warnes, Catherine Butler, Jasmin Pal, Nick Ayrest, Trish Corzine, Alice Keown, Kate Taylor, Josh Leon, Jonathan Moradoff, Theo Fordham, Ted Schama, Nick Weir, Vinu Bhatessa, Sheena Bhatessa, Neil Bhatessa, Natalya Manoukian, Sara Ammar, Mahdia Benbella, Jessica Saadat, Paul Saunders, David El-Ghanayan, Daniel Attia, Aziz Francis, Ali and Hussein Matar, Nick Duck, Simon Lawrence, Sarah Hung, Gabriel Murray, Keith Ward, Soufiane Bennis, Adil Loudiyi, Sasha Dayal, Dominic Pereira, Peppe Riviezzo, Raidan Al-Shaar, Houari Djahl, Tarek Meliti, Talal Alendari, Wassim Darwich, Ibrahim Dbouk, Salim Ladjici, Firas Marouf, Sulaiman Sousani, Fadi Chafi, Katarzyna Janiak, Simone Schaap, Tomasz Josko, Bassam Fattouh and Nikhil Timbadi. Thanks to all of our suppliers especially Abdu At Paxmead, Ihab at Patchi, and Wadih at Shadow on Thames.

Thank you to my dearest mother, Zohra, who is simply the woman of my life. To my brothers Madjid, Salah, Ramedane, Mehdi, and Mourad, and my only sister, Safia. Also to my nephews Karim, Rayan, Aymen, Chabane, Jibril, Adam, Sami, and Nail, and my nieces Imen, Meriem, Sabrina, Ines, and Soraya.

My brother-in-law, Halim, my sisters-in-law Sophie, Sandra, and Linda. To my grandmas Yamina (RIP) and Dhia (RIP), my uncles Arezki (RIP), Ali (RIP), Meziane, Omar, Ramedane, and Tayeb, and my aunts Cherifa (RIP), Mazouza, Saliha, and Malika, and my cousin Nassim (RIP) and all my 44 close cousins...

To all our team that works so hard to deliver our vision, day in day out, and who welcome our guests with the warmest hospitality and make the most delicious Lebanese food for all of our customers.

And to all of the wonderful customers who have been through our door — thank you for all your compliments and most importantly your honest feedback that helps us every day to improve your experience in our restaurants.

Tony

INDEX

This edition first published in hardcover in the United States in 2014 by
The Overlook Press, Peter Mayer Publishers, Inc.

141 Wooster Street
New York, NY 10012
www.overlookpress.com

For bulk and special sales please contact sales@overlookny.com,
or write us at the above address

Cataloging-in-Publication Data is available from the Library of Congress

First published in Great Britain in 2013 by Preface Publishing
An imprint of The Random House Group Limited

Typeset by Neal Townsend at Them Apples Design
Printed and bound in China by C&C Offset Printing
Additional images courtesy of Michael Franke and Ingrid Rasmussen

ISBN 978 1 4683 0957 7

10 9 8 7 6 5 4 3 2 1